Conversations at the
Frontier of Dreaming

Other Books by Thomas Ogden

Projective Identification and Psychotherapeutic Technique

The Matrix of the Mind: Object Relations and the Psychoanalytic Dialogue

The Primitive Edge of Experience

Subjects of Analysis

Reverie and Interpretation: Sensing Something Human

CONVERSATIONS AT THE FRONTIER OF DREAMING

BY

THOMAS H. OGDEN, M.D.

KARNAC

LONDON   **NEW YORK**

The author gratefully acknowledges permission from the following journals to reprint previously published material.
Chapter 2: 'Reverie and Metaphor: Some Thoughts on How I Work as a Psychoanalyst,' *International Journal of Psychoanalysis*, 78:719-732,1997 (Copyright © Institute of Psychoanalysis). Chapter 3: 'A Question of Voice in Poetry and Psychoanalysis,' *Psychoanalytic Quarterly*, 67:426-448, 1998 (Copyright ©The Psychoanalytic Quarterly, Inc.). Chapter 4: '"The Music of What Happens" in Poetry and Psychoanalysis,' *International Journal of Psychoanalysis*, 80:979-994, 1999 (Copyright © Institute of Psychoanalysis). Chapter 5: 'Borges and the Art of Mourning,' *Psychoanalytic Dialogues*, 10:65-88, 2000 (Copyright © The Analytic Press). Chapter 6: 'Re-Minding the Body,' *American Journal of Psychotherapy*, 55:92-104, 2001 (Copyright ©Association for the Advancement of Psychotherapy). Chapter 7: 'An Elegy, a Love Song and a Lullaby,' *Psychoanalytic Dialogues*, 11:293-311, 2001 (Copyright ©The Analytic Press). Chapter 8: 'Reading Winnicott,' *Psychoanalytic Quarterly*, 70:299-323, 2001 (Copyright ©The Psychoanalytic Quarterly, Inc.).

The author also gratefully acknowledges permission to reprint:
The poems from *The Poetry of Robert Frost* edited by Edward Connery Lathem. Copyright © 1941, 1942 by Robert Frost, ©1970 by Lesley Frost Ballantine, ©1928, 1969 by Henry Holt and Company, LLC. Reprinted by permission of Henry Holt and Company, LLC. 'The Snow Man' from *The Collected Poems of Wallace Stevens* by Wallace Stevens. Copyright ©1954 by Wallace Stevens. Used by permission of Alfred A. Knopf, a division of Random House, Inc. UK permission granted by Faber and Faber Limited. 'Song' from *Opened Ground: Selected Poems 1966-1996* by Seamus Heaney. Copyright ©1998 by Seamus Heaney. 'Epilogue' from *Day by Day* by Robert Lowell. Copyright ©1977 by Robert Lowell. Reprinted by permission of Farrar, Straus and Giroux, LLC. UK and British Commonwealth permissions granted by Faber and Faber Limited. 'Pierre Menard, Author of the Quixote' and 'Borges and I', translated by James E. Irby, from *Labyrinths* by Jorge Luis Borges. Copyright ©1962, 1964 by New Directions Publishing Corp. Reprinted by permission of New Directions Publishing Group. UK and Commonwealth permissions granted by Laurence Pollinger Limited. 'Clearances' from *Opened Ground: Selected Poems 1966-1996* by Seamus Heaney. Copyright ©1998 by Seamus Heaney. Reprinted by permission of Farrar, Straus and Giroux, LLC.

Published in UK 2002 by
H. Karnac (Books) Ltd.
6 Pembroke Buildings
London NW10 6RE

ISBN: 1 85575 906 3

Published in US by Jason Aronson Inc.
Library of Congress Cataloguing-in-Publication Data
Ogden, Thomas H. Conversations at the frontier of dreaming/ by Thomas H. Ogden
p.cm. Includes bibliographical references and index
1. Psychoanalysis 2. Psychoanalytic Counselling 3. Freud, Sigmund, 1856-1936 I. Title
BF173.O44 2001
154.3-dc21   00-052190

www.karnacbooks.com

To Richard Ogden,
my brother and lifelong friend

Contents

Yet why not say what happened?

Robert Lowell, "Epilogue," 1977

1

Conversations at the Frontier of Dreaming

This is a book of conversations: spoken, unspoken, and yet-to-be-spoken conversations between (and within) analysts and their patients; imaginary and real conversations (the imaginary ones, such as dreaming and reverie, being often the most real); wordless conversations between poets and the poems they make, and between poems and the readers they make; conversations between feelings and thoughts, and between thoughts and words; conversations between the inexpressible and the expressible, a distance mediated by metaphor, by the sounds and cadences of words and sentences, and by images and gestures (verbal and otherwise); and, of course, the conversation between us, reader and writer, a conversation that derives life from all of the other conversations, and imparts life to them.

And, as if by accident (but it is certainly not a matter of chance), the very word *conversation* is in conversation with itself, spawning metaphors as it goes. The word *conversation* is "fossil poetry" (Emerson 1844, p. 231), derived from the conjunction of the Latin words *cum*, meaning with or together, and *versus*, meaning a row or furrow of earth; the movement of a plough turning back on itself as it ends one row and begins the next; and a line of poetry or other writing. *Conversation* is a word that has preserved in itself a chorus of accumulated meanings that speak both from the experience of opening the earth for purposes of impregnating/planting and from the experience of entering into language for purposes of communicating with ourselves and others. Thus, conversation is an act of engaging with another person in the work of creating man-made lines, lines of furrowed soil reflecting mankind's timeless effort to survive by taming and freeing the earth and Nature. At the same time, conversation is an act that reflects man's equally timeless effort to tame and to free himself (his own human nature) by transforming raw experience into words and gestures to communicate with others and with himself. There is nothing more fundamentally, more distinctively human than the need to converse. As innumerable observational studies of infants have demonstrated, we depend for our lives upon conversation (both in terms of our physical survival and in terms of our coming humanly to life).

In the history of psychoanalysis both as a theory and as a therapeutic process, few conversations have played a more central role than the one entailed in the experience of dreaming. The internal conversation known as dreaming is no more an event limited to the hours of

(links to Bion's theory)

sleep than the existence of stars is limited to the hours of darkness. Stars become visible at night when their luminosity is no longer concealed by the glare of the sun. Similarly, the conversation with ourselves that in sleep we experience as dreaming continues unabated and undiluted in our waking life.

The unconscious conversation that in sleep we experience as dreaming, in the analytic setting we experience as reverie. The analyst's reveries are his waking dreams. Reverie may take almost any form, but most often, in my experience, it presents itself obliquely to awareness in the most unobtrusive, quotidian of forms: as ruminations, daydreams, sexual fantasies, snippets of films, "audible" musical phrases or lines of poetry, bodily sensations, and so on.

The psychoanalytic frame (for instance, the use of the couch) and psychoanalytic technique (for instance, the free associational method used by both analysand and analyst) are designed to enhance the capacity of each participant to achieve a state of mind in which he might gain access to the continuous unconscious conversation with himself that takes the form of dreaming in sleep and of reverie in waking life. The analyst's reverie state involves a withdrawal from the logic, demands, and distractions of external reality that is analogous to the "darkness" of sleep (the insulation of the mind from the glare of consciousness)—a darkness in which dreaming, a continuous psychic event, becomes perceptible. As Freud (1916) put it, "I have to blind myself artificially in order to focus . . . on one dark spot" (p. 45). The analyst's rev-

(handwritten margin note): Is this what C is doing when she sets upon a particular direction in the dream e.g what is the man (already described as silloete) wearing? Or, would you like to put the baby to your breast.

(handwritten bottom note): → Assignment thought...
→ Healing when asking what would you like to say to that person? what needs to happen to make it better? What would it be like if you said how you feel / said no?

erie state is his waking sleep or sleeping wakefulness, a state in which he looks darkly into the productions of the unconscious. As one matures as an analyst, one's eyes more readily become "adapted . . . to the dark" (Freud 1916, p. 45).

In recent years, to my surprise, I have found that a set of metaphors introduced by Freud more than a century ago provides a fresh language and imagery with which to think and speak about the reverie experience of analysts, and the techniques we as analysts use to facilitate our awareness of that experience. (All metaphors break down at some point, and, as we shall see, this "newly discovered" set of metaphors is no exception.) I am referring to Freud's topographic model (adumbrated as early as 1896, but not fully developed until 1915), in which he conceived of the mind as having three "parts": the conscious, the preconscious, and the unconscious minds. (I picture the preconscious mind in this model as an oval lying between two large open-ended parabolic shapes opening outward. The conscious mind is represented by the parabola in the upper right corner of the imaginary page, and the unconscious mind by the parabola in the lower left.)

By the terms of this topographic model, there are two "frontiers" (Freud 1915, p. 193), one between the preconscious and the conscious mind, and the other between the preconscious and the unconscious mind. The "business" conducted across the preconscious-conscious frontier is largely a matter of the intentional shifting of the individual's attention from one point of interest to another. Consciousness requires an uncluttered "perceptual surface"—the metaphor is beginning to creak—with which to register current, ever-changing external reality; it also requires access to memory (memory acceptable to consciousness) so that present experience may be contextualized and informed by past experience. Past experience conserved in the preconscious "storehouse" of memory is segregated from conscious awareness so as not to overcrowd the conscious mind, and yet is fully accessible to conscious thought. For instance, we do not keep our telephone numbers continuously in conscious awareness, but we can "bring them to mind" if we direct our attention to them.

My principal interest, though, is in that other metaphorical frontier, the one between the unconscious and the preconscious minds. I believe that it is not hyperbole to say that the psychological work that occurs at the frontier between the preconscious and unconscious minds is at the very core of what it means to be alive as a human being. That frontier is the "place" where dreaming and reverie experience occur; where playing and creativity of every sort are born; where wit and charm germinate before they find their way (as if out of nowhere) into a conversation, a poem, a gesture, or a facial expression; where symptomatic compromise formations are generated and timelessly go on haunting us and sapping vitality from us as they provide order and the illusion of safety at the cost of freedom.

That frontier between the unconscious and preconscious—the frontier of dreaming—is the metaphorical

place of that distinctively human conversation with ourselves in which raw experience that simply is-what-it-is
(Bion's [1962] "beta elements" and Freud's [1933] "*das
Es*," or "the it") is transformed into experience that has
accrued to itself a modicum of the quality of "I-ness":
that is, of self-reflective awareness mediated at least in
part by verbal symbolization. This transformation is, I
believe, what Freud had in mind in his famous dictum,
"*Wo Es war, soll Ich werden,*" "Where it was, there I shall be
becoming" (poorly translated by Strachey as "Where id
was, there ego shall be" [Freud 1933, p. 80]).

A caveat is necessary here, lest the psychological work
done at the frontier of dreaming be thought of as a linear
"forward" progression from unconscious to preconscious,
from it-ness to I-ness, from thing-in-itself experience to
higher-order symbolization and reflective self-awareness.
Such a linear conception badly misrepresents the psychological work to which I am referring, which is most fundamentally dialectical in nature. (The term *dialectical* seems
apt given its derivation from the Greek word *dialektos*,
meaning discourse.) Unconscious experience and preconscious experience, "it-ness" and "I-ness," raw sensory experience and verbally mediated experience, are all without
meaning except in relation to one another; and, once differentiated from one another, they continue throughout
life to stand in conversation with one another, each creating, negating, preserving, and vitalizing the other.

The frontier of dreaming, as I am conceiving it, is a
psychological field of force over-brimming with freeing,
taming, ordering, turning-back-on-itself, impregnating,

"versifying" impulses. The versifying impulse is the impulse toward symbolic expression generated not only by the unceasing striving of the unconscious for conscious expression, but also by the phenomenon of "consciousness run[ning] to meet it [the unconscious] on all occasions" (Andreas-Salomé 1916, p. 42). For instance, we feel somehow cut off from ourselves when for a period of time we are unable to remember our dreams, or find ourselves unmoved by music, poetry, painting, humor, lively conversation, or any of the other sorts of creative expression that once held the power to touch us deeply. But I am less concerned at this point with the product of the creative act that emanates from conversation at the frontier of dreaming (e.g., the dream, the poem, the drawing) than with the experience of the impulse toward symbolic expression. The moment prior to speaking or drawing or dreaming is not a moment of affectless waiting; it is a moment alive with the desire, the impulse, the need to give voice to the inarticulate. It is a form of aliveness not found in speech itself, for once the words have been spoken (the dream dreamt, the line drawn), the impulse toward symbolic expression has been spent and, in a sense, killed. The frontier of dreaming is crackling with the impulse toward symbolic expression. It is a space "utterly empty, utterly a source" (Heaney 1987, p. 290), a place where the moment of creativity is sustained as "an imminence . . . never fulfilled" (Borges 1981, p. 39), a place where "all nominative cases must be replaced by the case indicating direction, the dative" (Mandelstam 1933, p. 284).

Paradoxically, the uniquely human experience of symbolically mediated self-consciousness that is generated at the frontier of dreaming is powerfully shaped and colored by what lies outside of conscious awareness. Self-consciousness is brimming over with bodily urges, impulses, cravings, and sensations lurching toward satiation, and at the same time driven by the need to know and to think and to enter into life experience mediated by language. The metaphor of the frontier of dreaming, in this light, refers to a dialectical field of force generated by the collision of desire, the need to know one's desires, the drive to give personal expression to them, and the need to have those expressions of desire recognized and responded to (by oneself and by others). Human desire is created *qua* desire by the need to know one's desire and to name it and to give expression to it; conversely, the need to know, to speak oneself, and to be known by others and met with "original response" by them (Frost 1942a, p. 307) is created in direct response to the pressure of one's desires.

At the frontier of dreaming, the dreamer who dreams the dream is in conversation with the dreamer who understands the dream (Grotstein 2000). Freud's dream-work, the individual's desire seeking symbolic expression in the act of making a dream, is in conversation with the "understanding-work" (Sandler 1976, p. 40), the individual's unconscious need to understand (that is, to recognize and creatively engage with his own expression of his needs, fears, and desires). The psychological events at the unconscious-preconscious frontier are to a large extent, though not entirely, unconscious (that is, under repression). That we are able to remember some of our dreams upon waking, and are able to hold onto a portion of our reverie experience before it slips from awareness, reflects the fact that these conversations with ourselves at the frontier of dreaming manage, as a consequence of the psychological work being done (which includes the creation of adequate disguise), to free themselves from the grip of repression. And yet, these remembered dreams and reveries live always in dialogue with what remains repressed: "the entire . . . gesticulating disquiet of those reduced to silence" (Andreas-Salomé 1916, p. 42).

From the perspective from which I have been speaking thus far, psychoanalysis might be thought of as a form of human relatedness specifically designed to create conditions in which the conversations with oneself that take place at the unconscious-preconscious frontier might be rendered increasingly "audible" to analyst and analysand. While I believe this to be true, I also believe that this depiction of the psychoanalytic enterprise is incomplete until we add the idea that the dreams and reveries being generated by analyst and patient at the frontier of dreaming draw not only on the unconscious experience of analyst and analysand as individuals, but also involve a set of unconscious experiences jointly, but asymmetrically, constructed by the analytic pair. This unconscious intersubjective construction (which I have termed "the analytic third" [Ogden 1994a]) is "the subject of analysis": a third subject with a life of its own, generated by the analytic pair and standing in dialectical tension with patient and analyst as separate individuals. It is disconcerting, to say the least, to recognize that our experiences of dreaming and reverie, which constitute a good deal of what is most personal to and self-defining for us, can no longer be viewed exclusively as our own individual creations. Our dreams can no longer be viewed as entirely our own. Instead (or, more accurately, in addition), the analyst's (and the patient's) dreaming and reverie are dreams of the jointly but asymmetrically constructed analytic third. An important implication for technique that follows from this understanding of dreaming is the notion that the analyst's associations to the patient's dream are no less important than the patient's associations to "his" dream. Conversations at the frontier of dreaming are not always private.

The analyst's use of his reverie experience, his waking dream-life, is indispensable to the analysis of the intersubjective analytic third. Since the jointly but asymmetrically constructed (and individually experienced) analytic third is dynamically unconscious, it cannot be invaded by sheer force of will. Instead, the analyst must adopt indirect associational methods in working with derivatives of what is happening unconsciously between himself and the patient (just as Freud [1900] developed his own undirected free association technique to "catch the drift" [Freud 1923, p. 239] of the unconscious in his own, and later in his patients', dream experience). For the analyst, an indispensable source of experiential data concerning the leading unconscious transference-countertransference anxiety at any given moment in an analytic session is available in the form of his reverie experience. Part of what makes the analyst's reverie experience so difficult to work with is the fact that it is not "framed," as dreams are framed, by waking states. Reverie experience seamlessly melts into other more focused psychic states. The analyst's reveries usually feel to him like an intrusion of his own current fatigue, narcissistic self-absorption, preoccupations, unresolved emotional conflicts, and so on. Despite these difficulties, I find that my reverie experience serves as an emotional compass that I rely on heavily (but cannot clearly read) in my effort to gain my bearings about what is going on unconsciously in the analytic relationship.

Treating my reveries as a waking dream-life that draws not only on my own unconscious experience, but also on the unconscious experience co-created with the analysand, is fundamental to my conception of the psychoanalytic process. As an analyst, I am

> not so much looking for the shape
> as being available
> to any shape that may be
> summoning itself
> through me
> from the self not mine but ours.
> (Ammons 1986, p. 61)

Poetry and fiction have become increasingly important to me over the years, not only as sources of pleasure, but also as sources of disturbance. These experiences with poems and fictions are an integral part of who I am in every sector of my life, including my ongoing effort to become a psychoanalyst. In this volume, I will attempt to convey a sense of how living (being alive) at the frontier of dreaming is not only an art, but the lifeblood of art itself. Although we all dream (both in sleep and in waking), not all dreams and reveries are equally artful. The success of art reflects the success of the individual in bringing his artistic medium to life and his life to his medium, whether that medium be lines of charcoal or lines of tilled soil or lines of poetry. In terms of the present discussion, the life—the vitality—of our dream life (and every other aspect of being alive) can be thought to reflect the fullness of the conversation with ourselves at the frontier of dreaming. I sometimes think of the outcome of an analysis, in terms of the degree to which analysand (and analyst) come to be able to carry on richer, more interesting, livelier conversations with themselves (both in sleep and in waking life), and consequently with each other. Or is it the other way around? Is it the enhanced richness of the conversation between analyst and analysand at the frontier of dreaming that enriches the conversation that each has with himself? Of course, we need not choose between the two.

2

Reverie and Metaphor

Some Thoughts on How
I Work as a Psychoanalyst

T. S. Eliot said of good writing, "We cannot say at what point technique begins or where it ends" (Pritchard 1994, p. 11). I think something similar could be said of psychoanalysis when it is going well. It is not staged, pre-scribed, or formulaic. But it is far easier to say what it is not than what it is. To explain to oneself how one works as a psychoanalyst, how one conceives of what one is doing in the consulting room, and what one aspires to in one's work is a lifelong task. What follows is part of that ongoing, always tentative, always incomplete dialogue with myself. The loosely knit "excerpts" from that dialogue that I will present here address specific aspects of psychoanalytic work, and in no sense comprise a comprehensive, balanced statement of a theory of technique. Rather, the thoughts presented are heavily weighted in the direction of aspects of analytic technique and practice that are currently of most interest to me (perhaps because I understand them least well).

I.

In any given analytic interaction, a compelling argument could be made for a variety of understandings of what is occurring, and an equally varied array of possible responses on the part of the analyst could be defended. A critical aspect of the way I locate myself among the possible understandings and responses involves my effort to attend to my sense of what, if anything, feels most alive, most real, in what is transpiring. The words "alive" and "real" are always in motion, always "on the wing" (James 1890, p. 253), and seem to defy, as if willfully, attempts to define and delimit their meanings. Despite this (or, more likely, because of it), I find these words useful in describing a quality of immediacy and vitality of personal experience upon which I rely in my attempts to talk to myself and to the analysand about what I sense is going on between us.

I believe that the development of an analytic sensibility centrally involves the enhancement of the analyst's capacity to feel in a visceral way the alive moments of an analytic session; to hear that a word or a phrase has been used, "lit again" (Bialik 1931, p. 135), in an interesting, unexpected way; to notice that a patient's glance in the waiting room feels coy or apologetic or steamy; to sense that a message left on one's answering machine feels dangerously, and yet alluringly, mysterious; to experience in a bodily way that a period of silence in the hour feels like lying in bed with a spouse whom one has loved for many years, but who now feels like a stranger.

In my efforts to make use of my experience in the analytic relationship, an enormous difficulty presents itself: much if not most of my feeling experience while with an analysand is not initially a part of my conscious awareness. It is here that one of the fundamental paradoxes of analytic practice lies. In order to do analytic work, the analyst must be able to experience and talk with himself (in as full a way as possible) about what it feels like being with the patient; and yet, for the most part, these experiences are unconscious. The analyst is initially, and for quite a long time, more "lived by" these predominantly unconscious feelings than he is the author of a set of thoughts, feelings, and sensations that he experiences as his own creations and can name for himself. A good deal of my work as an analyst involves the effort to transform my experience of "I-ness" (myself as unselfconscious subject) into an experience of "me-ness" (myself as object of analytic scrutiny).

To complicate matters still further, it has increasingly seemed to me that my experience of each analytic situation is to a very large degree a reflection of the specific type of unconscious intersubjective construction that the patient and I are in the midst of creating. The sort of unconscious engagement with the analysand to which I am referring results in the creation of a third subject, the "intersubjective analytic third" (Ogden 1994a, b, c, d, 1995, 1996a, b, 1997a, b). The experience of analyst and analysand in (and of) the analytic third represents an experiential base, a pool of unconscious experience to which analyst and analysand both contribute and from which they individually draw in the process of generating their own experience of the analytic relationship.

From this perspective, it is no longer self-evident what we mean when we speak of the analyst's or the analysand's "own" feelings or even the patient's "own" dreams and dream associations (Ogden 1996b). At the current moment in the development of psychoanalytic thought, we are aware of and must struggle with the complexity of the dialectic of individuality and intersubjectivity. To paraphrase and extend Winnicott (1960), we must live with the paradox (without attempting to resolve it) that there is no such thing as an analysand apart from the relationship with the analyst, and no such thing as an analyst apart from the relationship with the analysand. At the same time, from another perspective, there are obviously an analyst and an analysand who constitute separate physical and psychological entities. Consequently, a principal task faced by the analyst is to recognize and make use of the largely unconscious feeling states generated intersubjectively in the analytic relationship. The importance of the analyst's close attentiveness to the nuances and details of the events in the analytic hour is a well-established facet of contemporary analytic thought (Gray 1994).

In addition, however, I feel that it is necessary for analysts to further develop indirect methods for "catching the drift" (Freud 1923, p. 239) of the unconscious dimensions of the analytic relationship just as Freud (1900) in *The Interpretation of Dreams* found it necessary to generate indirect (associational) methods by which to gain access to the latent (unconscious) content of his own dreams. For me, an indispensable avenue in the effort to get a sense of my unconscious experience in and of the analytic third is the use of *reverie* (Bion 1962). As I mentioned earlier, I include in the notion of reverie the most mundane, quotidian, unobtrusive thoughts, feelings, fantasies, ruminations, daydreams, bodily sensations, and so on that usually feel utterly disconnected from what the patient is saying and doing at the moment (Ogden 1997a).

Reverie, like the manifest content of dreams, is an aspect of conscious experience that is intimately connected with unconscious experience. One must struggle to "hold on to" one's reverie experience before it is "reclaimed" by the unconscious. This struggle is not only a struggle with the forces of repression. Because our reverie experience is so large a part of our almost invisible background sense of self, it is equally a struggle with the wish/need for "the privacy of the self" (Khan 1974). A reverie that has at one moment seemed fully available to conscious awareness will frequently at the next moment seem to have "disappeared," leaving only a nonspecific residue of feeling in its wake.

Thus the analyst's use of his reverie experience is in my view a central component of analytic technique (Ogden 1995, 1996b, 1997a). Although it is beyond the scope of this chapter to offer a detailed clinical discussion of the way I attempt to make use of reverie in the analytic setting, perhaps the following brief (highly schematized) clinical vignette may be of value in conveying something of the experience of reverie and its role in

the analytic process. (For detailed clinical presentations
of my use of reverie experience, see chapters 4 and 6.)

> In a recent hour, an analysand, Mr. W, told me with
> a great deal of intensity of feeling how much it fright-
> ened him to be as "mentally out of control" as he is.
> Mr. W had been twice married and twice divorced,
> each time leaving his former wife with children from
> whom he felt estranged. He said that I was the only
> person to whom he had revealed the full extent of
> his "craziness." As Mr. W was speaking, my mind
> "wandered" to thoughts about my upcoming fifti-
> eth birthday. I recalled a recent conversation with a
> friend in which I had half-jokingly said that I was
> "handling" turning fifty by refusing to believe it. The
> "joke" in retrospect felt like a self-conscious attempt
> to be witty. I seemed to have been trying too hard,
> and I felt embarrassed as I went over the conversa-
> tion in my mind. As I refocused my attention on
> what Mr. W was saying, I attempted to consider my
> reverie in the context of what was going on in the
> analytic relationship. After a while, I said to Mr. W
> that, while I thought he felt genuinely frightened of
> the degree to which he feels crazy and out of con-
> trol, I had the sense that at other times (and per-
> haps even now), he succeeds in making that sense
> of himself so unreal to himself that he does not be-
> lieve it to be a part of who he is. Mr. W was silent for
> a few moments, and then he said (in a way that was
> noticeably less pressured than before) that when he

talks about analysis as if it were "an elective thing" for him, his "craziness" feels like something from the distant past or maybe even something happening to somebody else whom he knows well, but who is not entirely him. "It's not that I really think of it as another person, but it doesn't feel like me."

In this clinical situation, I was able to make use of a seemingly unrelated set of feelings and thoughts that I "recalled" during the session with Mr. W. (The word *recall* is somewhat misleading here in that the thoughts and feelings involved in the reverie did not constitute a mental repetition of something that had already occurred; rather, these thoughts and feelings constituted a new event created in the context of the analytic relationship as it was consciously and unconsciously evolving at that moment.) Thoughts and feelings about my upcoming fiftieth birthday had occurred with a number of patients that I was seeing during that period. In each instance, however, the images, thoughts, feelings, and sensations that were generated were contextualized by, and strongly reflected, the specific qualities of the conscious and unconscious constructions that were most pressing with each individual patient. In the session described, it seemed to me that the reverie concerning the "joke" about "handling" the birthday by refusing to believe it reflected my reliance on a form of splitting and omnipotent thinking that were designed to protect me from directly naming and fully experiencing the pain associated with the event.

Moreover, the cavalier quality of the "performance" seemed to claim victory over both my own feelings and the passage of time. The illusion of playfulness in the "joke" served to disguise the strained manic defenses that I was using so as not to experience the sadness and fear that were for me associated with turning fifty. It had been only a few days prior to her fiftieth birthday that my closest friend had learned of the wide metastatic spread of her breast cancer. The feeling of embarrassment in my reverie (the awareness of my transparent effort to be clever) seems to me in retrospect to have been a reflection of a feeling of embarrassment about my wish to evade the fear associated with the recognition and acknowledgment of my own mortality (which had become all too real) and the deep sadness I felt in connection with the death of a friend. I was only dimly aware of this aspect of my experience at the time in this analysis that I am describing.

The interpretation I offered placed emphasis on the emotional disconnection that I sensed in Mr. W's relationship to the aspect of himself that felt "crazy" and utterly outside of his control. Mr. W's response to my interpretation (his partial recognition of the way he often treats the psychotic aspect of himself as foreign) had a solemnity to it that began to convey something of the depth of fear and sadness tied up with his experience of this largely split-off psychotic aspect of himself. It did not, however, reflect to any significant degree a sense of responsibility and guilt concerning the destructive effects of his "craziness" on his former wives, his children, the analysis, or me. I suspected, on the basis of the feeling of embarrassment in my own reverie, that feelings of shame or guilt might shortly become a discernible element of the transference.

II.

The aspect of analytic work to which I will now turn involves the attempt to be attentive to use of language—my own and the patient's—in the hour. I experience this aspect of analytic work not as a burden to be carried, but as one of the great pleasures of being an analyst. Analyst and analysand largely rely on indirect (symbolic) methods of communicating (primarily through the use of language) to convey to each other something of what they are feeling. In attempting to use words in this way, the patient is not so much telling the analyst what he feels as he is showing him and telling him through his use of language what he feels *like*, and what he imagines the analyst feels *like*.

The names that we have for feelings—*fear, loneliness, despair, joy*, and so on—are generic labels for categories of feeling, and often in themselves convey very little of the speaker's unique individual experience in that moment. When a patient tells me that she felt despairing over the weekend, I may ask what her despair felt like. Or if she is a patient who has difficulty knowing what she feels or even where she feels it, I might ask, "How did you know you were feeling despairing?" or "Where in your body did you feel the despair?" In their efforts to inquire into, or to describe, what despair or loneliness or joyfulness feels *like*, analyst and analysand necessarily find themselves engaged in the use of metaphor. At almost every turn, I believe that we as analysts, in our own use of language, are unconsciously teaching and learning the value of the use of metaphorical language. Metaphor is an integral part of the attempt of two people to convey to one another a sense of what each is feeling (like) in the present moment and what one's past experience felt like in the past (as viewed from the vantage point of the present). As analysts, we are also involved in learning and teaching the *limits* of metaphor:

> All metaphor breaks down somewhere. . . . It is touch and go with the metaphor, and until you have lived with it long enough you don't know when it is going. You don't know how much you can get out of it and when it will cease to yield. It is a very living thing. It is as life itself. (Frost 1930, p. 723)

I have found that my interventions very frequently take the form of elaborating a metaphor that the patient or I have (usually unselfconsciously) introduced.

> In a recent analytic session, the analysand, Mr. H, said, "Last evening I didn't leave the college [where he teaches] with anyone. While waiting for the bus, I was completely alone with myself." I asked, "What was it like being alone with yourself? What kind of company were you for yourself?" The patient replied, "I don't know. I finished almost all of my Christmas shopping yesterday."

I commented that Mr. H had responded to my question by saying that he didn't know what sort of company he is for himself. I added that it seemed that he had gone on to suggest indirectly that the reason he didn't know was that he anxiously turns to activities like Christmas shopping to occupy the space in which he might feel what it is like to spend some time with himself. Later in the session, I returned to the metaphor in a slightly altered form. I said to Mr. H that in the same way that he regularly feels unwelcomed by me, he seems to experience himself as an unwelcome houseguest whom he distracts with activities in his hope that the virulence of the guest might be deflected, at least for a while. (My use of the word *virulence* was unexpected as I heard myself say it. It derived in part from many earlier discussions of the patient's experience of his father's savage verbal attacks on the patient and the cruelty of the patient's assaults on himself.)

The patient then said that he had not slept well for several months as a result of mechanical noises (the elevator and the heating system) in his apartment building. Drawing upon many previous discussions of the patient's experience of his own deadness and the deadness of the analysis, I commented that the mechanical noises that won't let him sleep may feel to him like disturbing dead (mechanical) aspects of himself that he is forced to hear and feel at night when he is less shielded by the "white noise" of "Christmas shopping." Mr. H was

then quiet for almost a minute, in what seemed to
me to be the first time in the session that he had
been able to diminish his reliance on the masking
effects (the white noise) of uninterrupted talk.

In this brief exchange, the patient introduced the
metaphor of being two people ("I was completely alone
with myself"). I then made his metaphor more explicit,
and attempted to make the language of the metaphor
more concrete and thus more recognizable as a fantasy,
by asking, "What kind of company are you for yourself?"
Mr. H then showed me another aspect of what kind of
company he is for himself, by brushing off my question
and showing little interest in playing with the metaphor.
He spoke of finishing his Christmas shopping, which (as
we had often discussed in relation to similar kinds of
behavior) was a type of feverish activity that is designed
to create for him an illusion of aliveness when he feels in
danger of experiencing a sense of profound deadness.
    Later in the session, I attempted to interpret by
means of a slightly elaborated version of the patient's
metaphorical image of his being a particular sort of company for himself. I introduced the metaphor of one aspect of the patient feeling like an unwelcome guest in
the house of another aspect of himself. I said to Mr. H
that I thought that he tries to keep the unwelcome
houseguest (his own sense of deadness) at bay (dis-
tracted) by using feverish activity to fill the (metaphorical) space in which the deadness and loneliness might
be experienced. Mr. H then said that he had not been

able to sleep well for months because of the mechanical noises in the building. I heard this as the patient's unconscious extension of the interpretation/metaphor. He was saying that the deadened aspect of himself was like a mechanical (inhuman) noise—an intrusive presence allowing him no rest even when it is kept at a distance (in other parts of the building/in split-off aspects of himself). I then put the patient's unconscious extension of the metaphor into more explicit language and connected it with the metaphor of Christmas shopping. I said that I thought the mechanical noises of the building that disturbed him at night may feel to him like disturbing deadened aspects of himself that he is less able to block out at night with the white noise of "Christmas shopping." I experienced the silence that followed as a response to my interpretation, in that it seemed to reflect an enhanced capacity on Mr. H's part to experience what it felt like being with himself and with me at that moment without immediately drowning nascent feelings in a flood of words and ideas.

What I am trying to illustrate in this clinical example is not the organizing power of a particularly rich or imaginative set of metaphors. (The metaphors just described do not seem to me to be particularly artful.) Rather, I am attempting to illustrate how large a part of the way patients speak to their analysts, and analysts to their patients, takes the shape of introducing and elaborating upon one another's metaphors (cf. Ingram 1996; Meares 1993; Reider 1972). I hope it is clear that when I speak of the use of metaphors in the analytic dialogue, I am not referring to self-consciously "poetical" use of language. Ordinary language is replete with metaphor, albeit oftentimes either deadened in effect by overusage or hardly detectable as metaphor because it has become so much a part of the meaning of the word. For example, each time a patient speaks to us, or we speak to a patient, about feeling "under pressure," "tongue-tied," "worn out," "deaf," "torn," "divided," "racked with pain," "emotionally drained," "not giving a shit," and on and on, the patient and analyst are introducing metaphors that might be elaborated, modified, "turned on their ear," and so on. "The etymologist finds the deadest word to have been once a brilliant picture. Language is fossil poetry" (Emerson 1844, p. 231). A great deal of what goes on in any analysis that is "a going concern" (to use Winnicott's apt phrase) is in the form of analyst and analysand creatively and unselfconsciously playing a "verbal squiggle game" (Boyer 1997) with spontaneously invented or newly rediscovered metaphors.

To illustrate further both the ordinariness and the critical importance of this kind of game, I will briefly present two such events that occurred in the course of a single morning of analytic work.

> Referring to the patient's marriage, which had ended in divorce after fifteen years, I said: "From what you've told me, it seems that the marriage felt to you as if it never took off—as opposed to having crashed." The patient responded by saying, "It felt like I was just a passenger. I hate my passivity, the

way I can go blank for years on end. I just sat there as if I had no say in what was happening. I don't have to tell you about it—you see it for yourself every time I'm here." The patient in this example elaborated on my metaphor of the flight of a plane and added her own metaphoric imagery that centered on "sitting there" passively ("blankly") as a passenger. This new metaphor then became the "analytic object" to which the patient and I responded.

A second patient, describing what it felt like being with me, said: "It is as if there is a part of me that I leave outside on the sidewalk every time I come here. He waits there patiently and when I'm finished talking to you I meet him at the foot of the stairs and we become one person again." Of the myriad ways I might have experienced this metaphor, it felt most alive to me in that moment (in the twelfth year of the analysis) as an unconscious statement of the patient's valuing the experience of privacy even in the context of a relationship with me that felt intimate to him. I told the patient that I thought it was important to him that I understand that his feeling of leaving a guy out there on the sidewalk does not mean that what is happening between us today feels thin or unreal to him. He said, "I've never been able to explain to L (his wife of almost thirty years) in a way that she can understand that my not being with her 100% is not a prelude to my one day leaving her. It's what allows me to stay with her."

For this patient there was a very thin, often indiscernible line, between the feeling of "not being there" and the feeling that an element of privacy is necessary even while feeling alive and emotionally present with another person. The delicate interplay of privacy and emotional presence had occupied a good deal of the analysis. The patient's metaphoric statement and my response described here capture only one moment (and by no means a static resting place) in this patient's struggle to negotiate between fears of chilling isolation and fears of "falling into" another person.

Attempting to work with patients who are very concrete in their thinking and use of language is an experience of communication (or lack of communication) characterized by a paucity of metaphorical language (or more accurately, an inability on the part of the patient to experience a metaphor as a metaphor). For such patients, people, events, feelings, perceptions are what they are: a session canceled because of the analyst's illness is just that: a session canceled because the analyst was ill, no more and no less. The event is an event; it is not even felt by the patient to be his experience of an event (Segal 1957; see also Ogden 1986).[1]

---

1. Of course, not all analysands are equally interested in or capable of entering into play with words and ideas. Patients who are not so inclined often introduce their own forms of playing into the analytic setting: for example, in their sense of humor, or in their response to music recently heard or played, or to sounds occurring in the analytic session. I view playing, in all its varied forms, as metaphorical in the sense that play is grounded in the experience

A patient recently said that he would have to write one hundred times that he should always be aware of his own needs and not simply defer to the wishes of others. The patient was using this metaphor of repeated mechanical writing to describe an imaginary effort to alter his penchant for substituting the wishes and ideas of other people for his own. (Even the idea represented in the metaphor had a strikingly clichéd feel to it.) In this instance, the patient was using a metaphor in a nonmetaphoric way. He was not able to hear/experience the fact that his comparison (his way of thinking, speaking, experiencing, and so on) held a potential for richness that was being undermined by his (unconscious) fear of recognizing and considering the comparison that he had made. He irritatedly wondered why the analyst was making such a big deal over what was only a "figure of speech." The patient was unable to allow himself to hear that his metaphor might be an expression of his unconscious perception/fantasy that the way he attempts to make psychological changes is as ineffective and doomed to failure as are the punishments in grade school that attempt to effect

---

of bringing different aspects of one's experience into relation with each other in new and interesting ways. When a patient is unable to engage in play of any sort in an analysis, "*the work done by the therapist is directed towards bringing the patient from a state of not being able to play into a state of being able to play*" (Winnicott 1971a, p. 38; emphasis Winnicott's). In the terms I am using in this chapter, the therapist's attention is turned to the problems involved in the making of metaphor in the context of the analytic relationship.

change by the mechanical, repetitive writing of a resolution to stop some delinquent behavior ("I will not talk in class, I will not talk in class"). At a still more unconscious level, the patient might also be heard as saying that the analyst colludes in his doomed approach when he fails to help the patient find another way of attempting to think and speak for himself in his efforts to bring about psychological change.

A second example of the nonmetaphoric use of potentially metaphoric language occurred in the early stages of an analysis presented to me in consultation. The patient, a twenty-eight-year-old paralegal in a large law firm, had been speaking for several sessions about the possibility of beginning to use the couch. He began a session during this period by laying his coat on the couch. He then sat down on the chair used by patients and said, "At least *something* of mine is on the couch." He quickly went on to discuss events at work. The analyst refrained from interpreting the patient's ambivalent gesture; her experience with him had been that any effort to play with the metaphors that the patient introduced was experienced by him as an unbearable intrusion.

When the patient was three, his father left the family, and from that point on he had no further contact with his father. Beginning with the father's departure and continuing until he was twelve years old, the patient slept in the same bed with his mother. It was he, and not his mother, who finally decided that he should sleep in his own bed. The patient felt profound shame and embarrassment about the fact that he had slept with his mother for all those years, despite the fact that there had been no overt sexual behavior.

At the beginning of the session being discussed, the patient had unconsciously introduced a metaphor in which he (his coat) was in bed (on the couch) with the analyst/mother while at the same time safely in his own chair/bed. It seemed to me that for this patient the very act of juxtaposing and examining the relationship between the two "parts" of the metaphor was equivalent to the consummation of the incestuous wishes and fears being struggled with in the language and imagery of the metaphor ("At least something of mine is on the couch"). It also seemed that the patient regularly disrupted the process of recognizing the connection between the two elements of a metaphor that he had introduced (in this instance, the connection between the coat [his body] and the couch [the analyst's bed]). In fact, the patient seemed to be continually disrupting every sort of potential connection. In the analytic relationship, this was enacted in the form of being late and missing sessions, interrupting the analyst while she was speaking, suddenly changing the subject in the middle of a discussion, and so on. Outside of the analytic setting, the patient often broke off relationships precipitously, just as they were developing some intimacy. In the absence of a father (or a "father-in-the-mother" [Ogden 1987]) to prevent the consummation of the incestuous fantasy, the patient felt that it was squarely on his own shoulders to prevent the consummation (the bringing together of the elements) of the incestuous act.

In the course of the consultation, I suggested to the analyst that she and the patient might be involved in a projective identification in which she was unconsciously refraining from interpreting the patient's *metaphoric* act (his "laying" his coat on the couch) for fear of consummating an incestuous *sexual* act: one that both she and the patient imagined could be forestalled by keeping the elements of the metaphor from being "brought together" (experienced and viewed in relation to one another).

III.

With metaphor, we say one thing in terms of another, or as Frost (1930) liked to put it, metaphor is a way of "saying one thing and meaning another" (p. 719). Without metaphor, we are stuck in a world of surfaces whose meanings cannot be reflected upon. Self-reflective thought occurs when "I" (as subject) look at "me" (as object). Metaphor is a form of language in which I describe "me" so that "I" might see myself. In an important sense, naming and describing "me" metaphorically creates both "I" and "me" as interdependent aspects of human self-awareness (human subjectivity). In other words, the individual (as object) is invisible to the self (as subject) until metaphors for "I" are used to describe/

create "me" so that "I" can see myself. This is the mutually creating dialectic of "I" and "me." To put it still another way: "I" as subject do not exist until I can see myself ("me" as object); and the individual (like a tree falling in the forest) is silent/invisible unless there is a subjective "I" to hear and see it. The event that creates both "I" and "me" is an event mediated by language in general and by metaphorical language in particular. Consequently, in a very significant way, analytic work with patients who operate in a world of concrete (nonmetaphorical) experience involves an effort to help the patient to come to life in a new experiential form—a form characterized by a self-awareness mediated by language.

I believe that the analytic experience is in a fundamental way a process through which the capacity for self-consciousness is expanded and enriched. The importance of insight, from this perspective, lies, to a large degree, in the way it facilitates the transformation of self-experience into an object that can be "seen." Insight is thus not only a process by which self-understandings (involving formerly unconscious aspects of experience) are developed, but also an important vehicle for the substantiation of "me" as object and the simultaneous elaboration of "I" as subject. The process of the creation of self-consciousness through the making of symbols and metaphors with which to represent oneself and one's experience to oneself is a very great achievement and a gift of immeasurable importance to the analysand: self-consciousness developed and elaborated in this way comprises a good deal of what it is to be human.

IV.

From the vantage point delineated in the foregoing discussion, it is now possible to elaborate more fully some
of the reasons why I place such great emphasis on the
analyst's use of his reverie experience. Reverie is a process in which metaphors are created that give shape to
the analyst's experience of the unconscious dimensions
of the analytic relationship. Unconscious experience can
only be "seen" (reflected upon) when represented to
oneself metaphorically (cf. Arlow 1979; Edelson, J. 1983;
Edelson, M. 1972; Shengold 1981; Trilling 1940). Reverie
is a principal form of representation of the unconscious
(largely intersubjective) experience of analyst and
analysand. The analytic use of reverie is the process
by which unconscious experience is made into metaphors that represent unconscious aspects of ourselves
to ourselves.

In one of the clinical illustrations I offered earlier, I
"half-joked" that I was "handling" my fiftieth birthday by
refusing to believe it. In that example, I was (unconsciously) creating a metaphor for my experience of what
was going on between the patient and me. The thoughts
and feelings condensed in the half-joke represented a
new form that I was giving to the unconscious experience of the patient's and my own "handling" of that which
cannot be controlled (aging, dying, shame, feeling in-
sane). Both of us in our own ways had to that point been
"refusing to believe it." My use of my reverie was a way of
speaking to myself about unconscious experience in a

form that I could "hear" and "feel" and use to create linkages with other thoughts and feelings. I was using reverie experience as an avenue by which to gain access to, and create metaphoric meaning for, formerly unnamed (unconscious) experience in (and of) the intersubjective analytic third.

Like a dream, a reverie experience is not a "piece" of the unconscious or an aspect of unconscious experience that has come into "view"—i.e., into conscious awareness. This cannot happen, since unconscious experience is by definition experience that lies outside of conscious awareness.[2] The comments of P. W. Bridgman (1950), a Nobel Laureate in physics, on man's inability to imagine the structure of nature provides language with which to consider the relationship between conscious and unconscious experience:

> The most revolutionary of the insights to be derived from our recent experiments in physics [is] the insight that it is impossible to transcend the human reference point.

---

2. Freud often used the expression *Bewusstseinsunfähig* to describe the status of unconscious ideas relative to conscious ones. Although Strachey translated the word as "inadmissible to consciousness," he states in an editor's note that the word's "literal meaning is '*incapable* of consciousness' [and] ... could equally well be translated 'incapable of being (or becoming) conscious'" (1893–1895, p. 225 n. 1). From this perspective, the unconscious is "unthinkable" (outside of conscious awareness), not simply because it is unacceptable to conscious awareness, but because it is by its nature "incapable of being (or becoming) conscious."

... The new insight comes from a realization that the structure of nature may eventually be such that our processes of thought do not correspond to it sufficiently to permit us to think about it at all. ... We are now approaching a bound beyond which we are forever estopped from pushing our inquiries, not by the construction of the world, but by the construction of ourselves. The world fades out and eludes us because it becomes meaningless. We cannot even express this in the way we would like. (p. 157)

The unconscious, as conceived by psychoanalysis, constitutes a realm of experience into which we cannot go as a consequence of "the construction of ourselves." This is not to say that the unconscious as a system of meanings, needs, and desires does not directly affect us, any more than Bridgman would claim that the structure of nature does not affect us. Indeed, it (whether the structure of nature or the unconscious) *is* us and we are it.

The unconscious is not simply a kind of thinking and of organizing feelings regulated by a different mode of creating linkages (that is, the primary process mode of linking); rather, it is a form of experiencing that by its nature cannot be brought directly into conscious awareness. When we say that an experience that had once been unconscious has "become" conscious, we are not talking about moving something into view that had formerly been hidden behind the screen of the repression "barrier." Instead, we are talking about the creation of a qualitatively new experience, one that is not simply brought into the "view" of conscious awareness.

Since we can never consciously "know" or "see" unconscious experience, the transformations that create derivatives of unconscious experience (for example, the operation of the dream-work or the "reverie-work") are not creating new forms of unconscious experience; they are creating expressions of what unconscious experience *is like*. For example, a patient told me that he had had a dream in which he saw a tidal wave approaching, but could not move or cry for help. This rendering of his dream did not represent a glimpse into the patient's unconscious internal object world; it was a psychological expression of what the patient's unconscious experience was like. It is a metaphor. Dreams are metaphors, reveries are metaphors, symptoms are metaphors for the individual's unconscious experience. To the degree that we as analysts are interested in unconscious experience, we are students of metaphor. It is therefore incumbent upon us to develop an intimate familiarity with the workings of metaphor so that we may come to know something of its expressive power as well as its limits.[3]

---

3. In referring to the recognition of the limits of metaphor, I am speaking not only of the ability to recognize where a metaphor has broken down, but also the capacity to sense the point at which the patient or the analyst is grappling with experience that is inexpressible in language.

V.

In my efforts to describe for myself and for the reader how I work as an analyst, I must address the relationship between two critical aspects of the analytic process. From beginning to end of every analytic session, I am attempting to locate myself and the patient in relation to two overlapping aspects of experience: (1) my sense of what it feels like being with the patient at a given moment and (2) my sense of the leading anxiety in the transference-countertransference at that moment. Both of these facets of experience are initially to a large extent unconscious. In attempting to orient myself in relation to them, I depend heavily on my capacity to transform reverie (already a metaphoric expression of unconscious experience) into more usable forms: that is, into more verbally symbolic forms that can be considered, reflected upon, and linked (in both primary and secondary process modes) to other thoughts, feelings, and sensations.

When I speak to a patient about what I think is going on between us, I attempt to speak *from* my experience in (and of) my reverie as opposed to speaking to the patient *about* my reverie. What is of value to the patient is not an account of what the analytic relationship (including the leading transference-countertransference anxieties) feels like to me, but an account of what the relationship and its attendant anxiety feels like to *him*, and how that experience relates to other experiences (both real and imagined) that he has had with me and with other people in the course of his life. A direct statement of the metaphors that I have created in order to speak to myself about the experience of being with the patient is likely to rob the patient of an opportunity to create his own metaphors. This is no small matter since, as discussed above, what is occurring in the process of metaphor-making is the creation of the verbal symbols that "substantiate" (give shape and emotional substance to) the self as object ("me"), thereby creating symbols that serve as mirrors in which the self as subject ("I") recognizes/creates itself.

Balint, Bion, and Winnicott have all stressed the central importance to analytic technique of the analyst's not stealing "the patient's creativity [by] . . . knowing too much" (Winnicott 1971b, p. 57); of his being ever cognizant that "the answer is the misfortune or disease of curiosity—it kills it. . . . Answers [interpretations that pretend to be answers] are space stoppers . . . putting an end to curiosity" (Bion 1976, p. 22); of providing room for the patient "to discover *his* way to the world of objects—and not to be shown the 'right' way by some profound or correct interpretation" (Balint 1986, p. 180).

The analytic enterprise (in my view), relying heavily as it does on the experiences generated in the overlapping states of reverie of analyst and analysand, requires conditions that foster communication and privacy simultaneously (Ogden 1996b). Overlapping states of reverie can only evolve in a utilizable form (a form that can eventually be linked with words in a self-reflective process) in a setting in which the privacy of both analyst and analysand is respected and safeguarded. At the same time, the analytic use of reverie often involves a dialogue, a verbal exchange across that "most absolute [of] breaches" (James 1890, p. 226) that divides the thoughts and feelings of one person from those of another. The dialogue that takes place in psychoanalysis is different from all other human dialogues in that it is an exchange that takes as its "starting-point" (Freud 1914a, p. 16) the effort to effect psychological change by means of the exploration of transference experience and the anxieties (resistances) attendant upon it. It is this conception of the psychoanalytic enterprise to which I return again and again, as I wrestle with the question of whether a particular aspect of what I am doing at a given moment or in a given phase of analysis is of use in facilitating an analytic process.

In a previous contribution (Ogden 1996b), I have discussed the way in which three aspects of analytic technique (the use of the couch, the role of the "fundamental rule" of psychoanalysis, and the analysis of dreams) might be reconsidered from the point of view that the analytic process requires conditions that facilitate overlapping states of reverie in analyst and analysand. I will not repeat that discussion here, but I refer the reader to it as an illustration of how strongly the way I work with patients has been influenced by the ideas about reverie and metaphor developed in this chapter.

Concluding Comments

I will conclude this discussion (which does not aspire to be inclusive or conclusive) by bringing together some of the never resolved, generative tensions that I have alluded to in this chapter. It is in large part the generativity of these tensions that for me keeps the analytic experience alive and interesting. Among these generative tensions are the tensions between individuality and inter-subjectivity; between privacy and communication; between reverie and interpretation; between the use of language in the service of effecting psychological change and the pleasure taken in imaginative use of metaphoric language for its own sake; between attempting to accurately name thoughts and feelings and enjoying and valuing the "wonderful indirections" (Emerson 1844, p. 232) that the analytic dialogue inevitably takes.

To summarize, in this chapter I have presented parts of an ongoing internal dialogue concerning how I work as an analyst. I have described how I try to sense what is most alive and most real in each analytic encounter, as well as my use of reverie in my effort to locate myself in what is going on at an unconscious level in the analytic relationship. I view each analytic situation as reflecting, to a large degree, a specific type of unconscious intersubjective construction. Since unconscious experience is by definition outside of conscious awareness, the analyst must make use of indirect (associational) methods—such as the scrutiny of his own reverie experience—in his efforts to "catch the drift" (Freud 1923, p. 239) of the unconscious intersubjective constructions being generated. I view reveries (and all other derivatives of the unconscious) not as glimpses into the unconscious, but as metaphoric expressions of what the unconscious experience is *like*. In my experience, when an analysis is "a going concern," the analytic dialogue often takes the form of a verbal "squiggle game" (Winnicott 1971c, p. 3) in which the analytic pair elaborates and modifies the metaphors that the other has unselfconsciously introduced.

3

A Question of Voice

In this chapter, I address the question of voice in an effort to explore an aspect of listening and speaking that I believe to be pivotal to the analytic experience. Creating a voice with which to speak or to write might be thought of as a way, perhaps the principal way, in which an individual brings himself into being, comes to life, through his use of language. This conception of voice applies to all forms of language usage, whether in poetry, in fiction, in prose, in drama, in the analytic dialogue, or in everyday conversation.

There is a vast difference between thinking, on the one hand, and speaking or writing, on the other. In speech and in writing, one listens to oneself in a way that is different from the way one experiences one's own thinking. Wallace Stevens (recounted by Vendler 1984) has said that one thinks in one's own language; one writes in a foreign language. I believe that Stevens is referring to the way writing (and I would add speech) entails a quality of otherness that affords us an opportunity to hear how we come into being in the way we use language.[1]

Voice is a quality of experience that is very difficult to define, and I shall not attempt to do so except in the way I use the notion of voice in the course of this chapter. "We don't know what the voice on the page is, or how it got there, or how to improve it, but we just know when we hear it. The voice on the page [is] a mysterious process. . . . It [is] there, but it [is] a mystery" (Looker, quoted in Varnum 1996, pp. 192–193).

The idea of voice is neither synonymous with the idea of a "true self" (voice as one's authentic self finding expression in language) or a "false self" (voice as a series of masks and poses). In an odd way, voice has qualities of both at the same time, and might be viewed in addition as a medium for conscious and unconscious "experimentation" with the experience of self:

> Language . . . enables us, somehow, to seem to get outside ourselves and to assume positions we may or may not really believe in. Thus, we are able to speak almost in someone else's voice, to be insincere, to be ironical, to be sarcastic, to be, even, objective (whatever that means). (Baird 1968, p. 200)

_____

1. Of course, the use of language is only one of many avenues by which the individual achieves a sense of aliveness in his experience of himself.

From the perspective of Baird's comments, it is entirely possible to imagine speaking with, or hearing, a voice that sounds sincerely insincere (a voice that succeeds in being insincere) and another voice that sounds insincerely sincere (a voice that seems to attempt sincerity but has a hollowness to it). In the end, I believe that it is the *aliveness* of the voice created in one's use of language that is the measure of what is most real to both speaker and listener, writer and reader. Attending to the experience of aliveness and deadness in language seems to me a more fruitful way of approaching the question of voice than the more static notions of sincerity and insincerity, truth and deception (Ogden 1995, 1997c, 1997d).

In focusing on voice in this chapter, I have no illusion that I am introducing something new to the analytic discourse. Analysts have been listening to the way people sound from the time that Breuer invited Freud to listen to the strange, bewildering, disturbing sounds of the female patients whom he had been attempting to treat (see, for example, Appelbaum 1966; Balkanyi 1964; Brody 1943; Edelson 1975; Gabbard 1996; Meares 1993; Silverman 1982). Nevertheless, we as psychoanalysts are relative newcomers to the work of attending to voice in that our discipline is hardly a century old. Consequently, I believe we are well advised to turn for instruction (in listening to and speaking about voice) to the people who have for millennia listened closely to "the *living* sounds of speech" (Frost 1915, p. 687) and who have developed a capacity for capturing/creating voices with which to bring themselves to life. I am speaking, of course, of poets,

playwrights, novelists, essayists—and writers and storytellers of other genres. Perhaps if we listen to the ways
they go about creating life in language and bringing language to life, we may further develop our own ways of
listening to, and finding words to describe, how a person
in the analytic setting goes about bringing himself into
being in language.

In this chapter, I will listen closely to two twentieth-
century American poems in an effort to provide a sense
of what I mean by voice and how I make use of the concept. A poem, though itself an inanimate "thing," provides a living voice spoken to the reader and by the
reader—a voice that can engage the reader in a firsthand,
unmediated way. In reading these poems, the reader need
not take my word—or that of literary critics, or even that
of the poet—regarding what the voices in the poems feel
and sound like. The reader will hear for himself with his
own ears (and his own emotional responsiveness) the
voices with which the poems speak and with which he,
the reader, speaks the poems.

I have selected a poem by Robert Frost and one by
Wallace Stevens as ports of entry into the subject of voice.
I have chosen these poems not because they speak with
particularly well-defined voices, but because I am very
fond of them and welcomed the opportunity to spend
considerable time with them in the process of writing
about them. Both of these poets are masters of voice, and
in each of the two poems I am considering here the poet
creates interesting, subtly layered, often elusive, sometimes unnameable voices, which comprise a very large

part of what the poems are "up to." In discussing these poems, I will not be engaged in an effort to get behind the language to what the poem really "means"; instead, I will attempt to get deeply into the language and allow it to get deeply into me. In particular, I will be attempting to experience and to find ways of talking about what the language is doing: what sort of life is being created in the voices of the poem, in the sound and movement of the words and sentences being spoken, in "the music of what happens" (Heaney 1979a, p. 141).

A good deal of the experience of the voice in these two poems is accessible only by reading them aloud. The poems are made of the sounds of words "strung together" (Frost 1914a, p. 675) into sentences which in turn have their own sounds, "sentence-sounds" (p. 675). These sounds are best heard with the ear (not a metaphorical ear, but the actual ear) and felt as shapes in one's mouth and sensations in one's body as one says them aloud. One must spend a good deal of time with these poems in order to get a feel for them: "A poem would be no good that hadn't doors. I wouldn't leave them open though" (Frost, quoted in Pritchard 1984, p. 20).

I. An Eloquence So Soft

"Never Again Would Birds' Song Be the Same" (1942b), a poem first published when Frost was nearing seventy, is for me one of Frost's most beautifully crafted and subtly evocative lyrics. This sonnet creates a voice that encompasses a very wide range of human experience: a voice

that is unique to itself, while at the same time being unmistakably Frost.

Never Again Would Birds' Song Be the Same

He would declare and could himself believe
That the birds there in all the garden round
From having heard the daylong voice of Eve
Had added to their own an oversound,
Her tone of meaning but without the words.
Admittedly an eloquence so soft
Could only have had an influence on birds
When call or laughter carried it aloft.
Be that as may be, she was in their song.
Moreover her voice upon their voices crossed
Had now persisted in the woods so long
That probably it never would be lost.
Never again would birds' song be the same.
And to do that to birds was why she came.

The poem opens with the sound of good-natured
chiding as the speaker, with mock skepticism, talks of a
man who professes a far-fetched notion about birds that
he actually seems to believe. There is a slightly disowned
intimacy in the speaker's voice as he fondly and skepti-
cally marvels at the capacity of this man to believe the
unbelievable, and speak these beliefs from a place in himself where there seemed to be no doubt. There is a feeling that what he believes he "believes . . . into existence"
(Frost, quoted in Lathem 1966, p. 271). One can hear in
the voice the pleasure taken in knowing someone so well

over the years that even his old stories and quirky beliefs
have become signatures of his being.

As the poem proceeds, the metaphor of narrator
describing a man of strange but deeply held convictions
is "turned" in a way that serves to invite the reader gently
to take his own place *in* the metaphor as he becomes the
person to whom the "argument" is addressed, while the
speaker becomes the man holding these odd beliefs.

There is delightful playfulness and wit in the
speaker's voice as he invokes flawed cause-and-effect reasoning to "explain" events occurring in a metaphor: the
birds in the garden (of Eden), having listened to Eve's
voice all day long, had incorporated the sound of her
voice into their song (as if time played a role in the mythic
Garden). The strange "belief" in the creation of an
"oversound" (a wonderful neologism) becomes an experience that occurs in the poem itself: that is, in the
changes taking place in the sound of the poem's voice.
The oversound developing in the voice is a softer sound,
"crossed" upon the more witty and ironic voice of the first
five lines. In the lines that follow, we hear and feel the
interplay of sound and oversound:

> Admittedly an eloquence so soft
> Could only have had an influence on birds
> When call or laughter carried it aloft.

The phrase "an eloquence so soft," with its delicate,
repeated "s" sounds, speaks with such tenderness and
respectfulness and grace that it seems to float above the
hard "c" sounds of the words "could" and "call" and "car-

ried" in the lines spatially below it on the page. The experience created in the language of the poem—of softer sounds suspended above harder ones—anticipates the image of sounds of "call or laughter" being carried "aloft."

The poem is in constant motion, continually creating unexpected oversounds. The words "Could only have had an influence on birds" brings the poem back to earth (back from the mythic metaphor) with a humorous thud. The extra unstressed syllable in this line creates a rather awkward cadence that causes the voice to stumble a bit and finally fall into the final stressed syllable "birds." The effect is to playfully, mischievously transform these airy, mythical birds into poultry (for the moment). At the same time, the play on the words birds/bards conveys quite a different "tone of meaning." There is a suggestion in this wordplay that the eloquence of the music of spoken language (both present-day and ancestral) could only have had an influence on *bards*, people who incorporate the sounds they hear with their "deep ear" (Heaney 1988a, p. 109) into their own songs/poems as oversounds— more in their "tone of meaning" than in their words/ messages.

There is a surprising turn in the final six lines of the sonnet, which open on a subtly dissonant note:

Be that as may be, she was in their song.

In this starkly assertive single-line sentence, the open-ended conditionality of "would declare" (when? to whom? under what circumstances?) and "could himself believe" (how? why? if what?) are replaced by the conclusive tones of "Be that as may be." This phrase, in conjunction with the forced, flat certainty of the words "she was in their song," represents a marked shift in voice and introduces an unsettling awareness of a yet-to-be-defined source of emotional pain or danger that had been almost entirely absent in the playfulness of the voice up to this point. This anxious insistence is woven into more complex sounds in the succeeding lines:

> Moreover her voice upon their voices crossed
> Had now persisted in the woods so long
> That probably it never would be lost.
> Never again would birds' song be the same.

The voice here is a more personal voice, filled with the effort to hold onto what is most valued; it is reminiscent of the tone of the words "And what I would not part with I have kept" in Frost's (1942c, p. 305) "I Could Give All to Time." In "Birds' Song," what is most valued is a belief—a belief which in these lines is no longer a certainty—that poetry, that this poem, can speak with an "eloquence" that reaches so deeply into human feeling and experience that it alters language itself, and has persisted in the woods/words so long that "probably it never would be lost." The "eloquence," the ability of poetry to change the sound of language, is only as potent as is the ability of this poem to create the sounds of a unique voice that will never be lost to the reader.

The phrase "probably it never would be lost" quietly and unobtrusively conveys a remarkable depth of sadness. The word "probably" softly suggests a feeling of doubt, never openly acknowledged, about the permanence and immutability over time of the oversounds created in the course of a poem or of a life. Characteristic of Frost's poetry, the line-ending words "never would be lost," give the word "lost" the "final word." In so doing the language undercuts the claim for permanence in the very act of making it.

The voice in the line "Never again would birds' song be the same" has moved well beyond the wit and charm of the first part of the poem, and beyond the bald assertion "she was in their song." The line has the sound and feel of a memorial prayer. In these most delicate and unpresuming of words (that contain not a single hard consonant sound), a sense of the sacred is evoked—a deeply personal sacredness filled with both love and sadness. The strength of the voice in this line keeps the declaration free of sentimentality or nostalgia. The line conveys a sense of the poet's attempts, in his making of poems, to create and preserve in the sound of his words something of the sounds of the past voices that have been most important to him: the voices of the people he has loved; the voices of the poems that have mattered most to him; the changing sounds of his own voice in the course of his life (both in speech and in the poems that he has written); and the sounds of ancestral voices that are not attributable to any particular person, but are part of the language with which he speaks and from which he creates his own voice and his own poems.

Something else is happening in the sounds of the words in this line that is as disturbing as the feeling of

doubt regarding the permanence of "oversounds." The
sentence begins with the phrase "Never again," which
serves to underscore that past voices will never again be
heard, will never again be directly experienced. Those
people and the sounds of their voices are gone. What we
have as consolation for that loss is a remembrance of the
sound of their voices "crossed" on our own and on the
voice of the poet. The oversounds are reminders of what
has been lost, but they are not the past voices themselves.
Those voices will never again be heard.

The sound of the voice in this line, as it repeats
the title of the poem, seems to make a place for the
poem to end. But no, there is one more line, with the
feeling of a hastily added postscript, that captures what
William James (1890) might describe as "a feeling of
and" (p. 245):

And to do that to birds was why she came.

The voice in this final line is wonderfully unexpected. Seemingly tossed off as an afterthought, it
insists on being read quickly and more loudly than the
previous line. It is filled with hard "t" and "c" sounds that
seem to make an awful racket after the quiet elegiac
sounds that precede. But the effect of the final line is
anything but incidental to the process of creating the
delicately textured sound of the voice in this part of the
poem. The simultaneity of irony and wit and compassion
and grief in the voice here carries enormous emotional
force. The power of the line is in part attributable to
masterful timing. It is positioned as the second half of a

final couplet in the first line of which sadness and muted consolation and a sense of the sacredness of past voices have been tenderly and respectfully brought to life. The last line of the poem creates a voice that somehow encompasses the full distance that the poem has come. There is a feeling of pleasure in playing with the sounds and meanings of words that does not diminish the oversound of grief and loss that has accrued in the course of the poem. In these final ten monosyllabic words, the poem is pulled forcefully, but in a generously humorous way, back into the immediacy and informality of the sounds of everyday spoken words. The phrase "And to do that to birds" feels better suited to a description of ten-year-old boys startling pigeons in a park than to a depiction of the effects of poetry on the sound of language and of the sound of language on poetry. The final words "was why she came" compounds the effect by invoking a tenderly comic tautology in which Eve arrives on the scene in order to do a job (as a plumber might arrive at a house to clean out a drain).

The voice in "Birds' Song" succeeds in making the poem itself an experience, and not a description of an experience. We can hear and feel in the action of the voice the delight taken by the poet in using language inventively. There is constant movement in the voice as humor invades sadness and sadness invades humor. In its insistence on being "always on the wing . . . and not to be viewed except in flight" (James 1890, p. 253), the voice manages to be a great many things. It seems to find solace and even joy in hearing and making oversounds at the same time as it is filled with the sadness of its recognition that the voices of the people who have mattered most to the poet (as well as his own earlier voices and eventually this one) will persist *only* as oversounds. "But isn't that quite a lot?" the sound of the voice of the poem asks equivocally.

II. The Sound of a Few Leaves

Wallace Stevens (b. 1879) and Frost (b. 1874) were contemporaries in the sense that the period of their maturity as poets roughly overlapped, but as is apparent in "The Snow Man" (1923), Stevens created a twentieth-century American voice in poetry unlike anything encountered in Frost (or in the work of any other American or British poet to that point). Stevens, unlike Frost, is a "difficult" poet in Eliot's (1924) sense of the word: his narratives are fragmented, the tone of the voice is often difficult to determine, and he frequently "dislocate[s] language into his meaning" (p. 248).

A poem (and I think this is particularly true of Stevens's poetry) must initially and finally be taken as a whole. It must be allowed to be "intelligent / Beyond intelligence" (Stevens 1947, p. 311), a series of words and sounds and cadences that suggest (and do no more than suggest) meaning—and, as often as not, obscure and contradict that meaning as soon as it is suggested. The task of the reader as critic is to marvel at how a poem works—what the language is doing, as opposed to what it is saying (what it "means"). After listening to and look-

ing into what the language of the poem is doing, one must
throw it back in the water, as it were, and allow the poem
once again to move and breathe and live in its own terms
as a "creation of sound" (p. 311). "The Snow Man" was
included in Stevens's first volume of poetry, *Harmonium,*
published in 1923.

The Snow Man

One must have a mind of winter
To regard the frost and the boughs
Of the pine-trees crusted with snow;

And have been cold a long time
To behold the junipers shagged with ice,
The spruces rough in the distant glitter

Of the January sun; and not to think
Of any misery in the sound of the wind,
In the sound of a few leaves,

Which is the sound of the land
Full of the same wind
That is blowing in the same bare place

For the listener, who listens in the snow,
And, nothing himself, beholds
Nothing that is not there and the nothing that is.

"The Snow Man," although a single sentence, seems
to me to speak in a sequence of three quite different
voices, each building upon, complicating, and enriching
the others. The series of voices has the effect of dividing

the poem into three intermeshed parts, the first of which extends into the middle of line 7:

> One must have a mind of winter
> To regard the frost and the boughs
> Of the pine-trees crusted with snow;
>
> And have been cold a long time
> To behold the junipers shagged with ice,
> The spruces rough in the distant glitter
>
> Of the January sun;

"One must have a mind of winter" is a remarkable opening line. In the space of seven words, the poem establishes a voice of extraordinary poise and balance, of beauty and restraint. It is an intelligent, meditative voice that seems to be speaking to itself, hardly if at all cognizant of the reader's presence. The voice of the poem makes no effort to explain itself. There is a feeling as each line moves gracefully into the next that the reader is to refrain from questioning, clarifying, or paraphrasing and instead must simply "regard" and "behold" what is going on in the words and phrases and sounds as they create their effects. The quiet, serene voice moves slowly but not laboriously through each of the three carefully balanced eight-beat phrases of the first stanza and the even longer flowing measures of the second.

The syntactic form of the line "One must have a mind of winter" reminds me of Frost's (1923a) line "One had to be versed in country things" (from "The Need of Being Versed in Country Things," which was published

in the same year as "The Snow Man"). But the similarity
of form serves to underscore the vastly different tone of
the voice in each. In contrast to the solitary inwardness of
Stevens's line, Frost's seems to be patiently and kindly (albeit mischievously) mindful of the reader. Frost's voice in
"Country Things" (as in "Birds' Song") seems to invite the
reader to share in the pleasure of playing with words: for
example, in the play on "versed"/verse and in the experience of the welcoming ordinariness of the word "things."
The reader receives no such invitation from Stevens.

In the opening part of "The Snow Man," the reader
is at least as much taken by the beauty and subtlety of
what is happening in the language as by the beauty of
the images of the winter landscape. For instance, the word
"shagged" in the phrase "the junipers shagged with ice"
seems to sag in the middle under the weight of the guttural "g" sounds. It seems that no other word would have
sufficed. We can hear in the voice a poetic sensibility that
is quietly contemplative while at the same time closely
attentive to the way language is being used. Part of the
speaker's masterful use of language is felt in the soft
(mostly internal) rhyming going on in this part of the
poem. This unobtrusive rhyming serves to knit these lines
together tightly and give them a quality of powerful inevitability (which is not to say predictability). Examples
of this kind of internal rhyming include mind/pine/
time/ice, cold/behold/snow, winter/glitter/junipers,
and one/sun (which rhyme ties together the first and last
word of this part of the poem).

The clause "the spruces rough in the distant glitter /
Of the January sun" creates a haunting, otherworldly
effect, a sense of vast silence and stillness disturbed only
by a faint movement of light, of white glittering against
white. The word "rough" is unexpected, and seems not
to carry the usual denotation of coarseness—there is
nothing coarse about the voice in these lines. The word
"rough" here is newly created in the poem, and seems to
have more to do with being a part of a rough sketch, an
artistic form meant to capture an essence in a few strokes
of a brush or a pen (which is what the language of the
poem is *doing* here).

The winter encountered in the first part of "The
Snow Man" is a winter created in language, in the poet's
"mind of winter" (a mind thinking, feeling, sensing,
imagining), as opposed to a winter "out there." Of course,
every poem is made of words and not of snow and ice and
trees. But in this part of the poem, the voice is that of a
poet who, having experienced winter in an emotional and
physical way ("having been cold a long time"), has created in language a winter that is uniquely his own. The
opening portion of the poem is more an experience of
language being used in extraordinary ways than it is an
experience of bumping up against a sense of something
that simply is there, something that has been found and
not made. This relation to winter is similar to the experience depicted in Stevens's (1936) "The Idea of Order at
Key West" as the speaker listens to a woman singing about
the sea:

It may be that in all her phrases stirred
The grinding water and the gasping wind;
But it was she and not the sea we heard. (p. 129)

"The Snow Man" seems to transform itself into something quite different in the middle of the seventh line, where the second part of the poem (as I hear it) begins and where a new voice is created:

and not to think
Of any misery in the sound of the wind,
In the sound of a few leaves,

Which is the sound of the land
Full of the same wind
That is blowing in the same bare place

In line 7, one is struck by the way the words "and not to think" are tucked into the same line as the final phrase of the first part of the poem: "Of the January sun." By isolating and juxtaposing these two phrases, the words begin to "talk to each other" (Frost 1936, p. 427). A "January sun" is a man-made thing: the month of January is a human invention. Nature has its cycles and rhythms, but it does not count them or name them as people do with their clocks and calendars. Having been positioned next to the "January sun," the words "and not to think" seem to become something of an announcement of the cessation of thinking, of inventing, of imagining, of making things in one's mind with words. If the opening portion of the poem had been an experience of a "mind of winter" thinking, feeling, regarding, beholding, creating, it seems that what is now happening in the poem is an experience of "not to think." In other words, what occurs in this line, and in the remainder of the third and fourth stanzas, is what happens if one does not think (does not create in feeling and imagination) and instead listens to something that one has not made.

The words "not to think of any misery" recall the final stanza of Frost's (1923a) "The Need of Being Versed in Country Things," in which phoebes (small birds) have made a nesting place of the remains of a barn that has been abandoned for years (after the farmhouse was destroyed by a fire):

> For them there was really nothing sad.
> But though they rejoiced in the nest they kept,
> One had to be versed in country things
> Not to believe the phoebes wept. (p. 223)

The way negation is structured in the last line of Frost's poem allows the poet not only to "have it both ways" (that is, to create a simultaneity of statement and negation), but also to give a semantically "incorrect" understanding "the final word" by allowing the poem to end with the sadness of the sound of the words "the phoebes wept." Stevens does something similar in "The Snow Man" by beginning the second part of the poem with the words "and not to think." By leaving these words disconnected, both spatially and emotionally, from what

follows, what one is "not to think" (and feel) is "released"
from its moorings in the negation.

In this "headless" (that is, "not to think") part of the
poem, the experience of winter comes to life in the
accelerating force of the sounds and rhythm of these
phrases, and in the repetition and alliteration of the
words "sound" and "same."[2] Something has broken loose
here in a way that feels as if the poem is leading the poet.
There is a sense of a powerful forward movement in the
sound of the words

> . . . in the sound of the wind,
> In the sound of a few leaves,

> Which is the sound of the land
> Full of the same wind
> That is blowing in the same bare place

These words have vitality not primarily for the ways
they reflect the workings of a mind, "a mind of winter";
they are alive and vibrant because they capture a sense
of something outside of themselves, outside of words,
outside of thinking and feeling and imagining. The word
"leaves" carries a highly compacted set of meanings beyond the surface meaning of leaves from a tree. The word
alludes to the sounds and feelings of rapidly "leafing"

---

2. In "The Snow Man," sight seems to be tied up with thinking and
watching and creating in one's mind, while hearing (not surprisingly for an art form so rooted in sound) seems to involve a more
direct, unmediated form of connection with the perceived (un-
imagined, inarticulate) otherness of the world and of oneself.

through pages of a book (no longer reading the words), of "leaving"/abandoning/departing the world of the mind, of giving or being given "leave"/permission to release oneself from confinement, of discovering what one "leaves" oneself after giving up one's own inventions. This multiplicity of meanings is only subliminally perceived by the reader because the poem here is up to something quite different from experiencing pleasure in the play of the meanings of words.

The second part of the poem is not describing or "regarding" winter; it is creating a sense of the hard, opaque alterity of winter as the words seem to hurl themselves from the page in clumps with increasing force, reaching a crescendo in the three consecutively stressed line-ending words "same bare place." The poet seems here not to have prearranged where the poem is headed; instead, there is a feeling of wildness: "It [a good poem] finds its own name and it goes and finds the best waiting for it in some final phrase" (Frost 1939, p. 777). The "same bare place," the final phrase into which the poem in its second section hurls itself is "more felt than seen ahead like prophecy" (p. 777). There is nothing inevitable occurring in these lines.

The language in the middle portion of "The Snow Man" achieves the seemingly impossible: it manages to create a voice in the sounds and rhythms and movement of the words that is a voice not of the speaker of the poem, but of something outside of the speaker—outside of the speaker's mind of winter—that seems to be speaking *through* the speaker. The speaking voice of the poem becomes other to itself, almost as if the poem is happening to the poet. The sounds of words and the sounds of winter seem to be more heard than created by the "speaker" who is now more listener than speaker.

"The Snow Man" makes still another turn and speaks with still another voice in the final stanza, the third "part" of the poem. The poet (and the reader) having heard/experienced/felt the sound of the wind, have each become "a listener, who listens in the snow." One can feel the honor bestowed upon the genuine "listener":

> For the listener, who listens in the snow,
> And, nothing himself, beholds
> Nothing that is not there and the nothing that is.

The final stanza is pure abstraction. It is almost completely imageless: there are no pine-trees crusted with snow, no junipers shagged with ice, no spruces rough in the distant glitter of the January sun. The voice is virtually toneless, lacking even the meditative sound of the voice of the first section of the poem. It is as if the sounds of words themselves have all but disappeared: there are only three consonants in the final stanza that have even a modicum of hardness. And along with the "disappearance" of the sound of the words is a sense of the disappearance of the speaker: "There are words / Better without an author, without a poet" (Stevens 1947, p. 311).

In this part of the poem we hear the sound of words that seem to speak themselves. The "listener, who listens in the snow" having become only a listener, a sensibility of pure receptivity, "beholds / Nothing that is not there": that is, only what is there, outside of the imagination, outside of constructions in words. What remains for this listener is silence, inarticulate silence, "the nothing that is." Paradoxically, this silence—the sound (the voice) of "the nothing that is"—is a sound created in words, words used artfully and imaginatively. The language, while creating a "voice of nothing," is neither silent nor still. The poet cannot escape his dependence on the sounds made with words (and the spaces between the words) in his efforts to create the sound of "the nothing that is."

Perhaps there is a quiet irony in the words "the nothing that is," in that the phrase seems to suggest that "the nothing that is" is everything—that is, everything we have not concocted with our words and imaginations. But "to do that" to the ending of this poem, to find subtleties of irony and wit, to "pluck out the last secret of the poem by unearthing, if necessary, its seventh [type of] ambiguity" (Heaney 1988a, p. 132), is to do violence to a poem and to an experience that asks not to be figured out, not to be reduced, not to be understood.[3]

The poem is grammatically a sentence, but it does not stop, it does not even seem to end with the period at

---

3. I am reminded here of Bion's admonition to his analysand James Grotstein when Grotstein responded to one of Bion's interpretations by saying, "I understand." Bion calmly replied, "Please try not to understand. If you must, superstand, circumstand, parastand, but please try not to understand" (Grotstein 1990, personal communication).

the close of the final line; instead, it seems to open itself up still further by using as its final word the word "is"— the most inclusive and inconclusive of words. The poem does not have an end in part because it does not have a beginning or a middle. The poem does not "progress" from one part, or from one voice, to the next. None of the three voices of the poem creates a resolution or a transcendence of the other two. Each voice is a different sound created in the process of the poet's effort to do something with all that lies outside of words and imagination. There is a voice that makes exquisitely beautiful sounds and works in interesting and subtle ways, turning trees and snow into "junipers shagged with ice" and "spruces rough in the distant glitter / Of the January sun." There is a voice of a speaker swept up by the force of rhythms and sounds that are discovered and that discover him and that seem more to speak through him than to be spoken by him. There is a voice of a listener in the snow who hears the silence and speaks the silence and is the silence that remains before and after all is said and done.

A discussion of the voices heard in "The Snow Man" would be incomplete if it did not make mention of a fourth voice that runs through and encompasses each of the other voices. The fourth voice is almost impossible to capture in words, and yet it is there. One can hear it. It is the unique sound—the "touch and texture" of the way language is being used, the "watermarking" (Heaney 1980a, p. 47)— that makes this poem and the voices and the music it creates distinctively the work of Wallace Stevens.

III. Voice in the Analytic Setting

In the preceding discussion of "Never Again Would Birds'
Song Be the Same" and "The Snow Man," I have tried to
illustrate some of the ways a speaker (whether oneself or
another person) comes to life through the use of language. In reading a poem, there are two voices acting
upon one another: the voice of the speaker in the poem
and the voice of the reader experiencing and saying the
poem. Consequently, it is not easy to say whose voice one
hears as one reads or listens to a poem. The voice heard
or made is a voice that is neither exclusively that of the
poet nor that of the reader; it is a new and unique voice,
a third voice that is generated in the creative conjunction
of reader and writer. No two readers of a poem will create the same voice.

Similarly, in an analytic setting, analyst and analysand
together generate conditions in which each speaks with
a voice arising from the unconscious conjunction of the
two individuals. The voice of the analyst and the voice
of the analysand under these circumstances are not the
same voice, but the two voices are spoken, to a significant
degree, *from* a common area of jointly (but asymmetrically) constructed unconscious experience. I have spoken
of this intersubjective experience, generated by the unconscious interplay of analyst and analysand, as the "analytic third" (Ogden 1994a). In a sense, the "oversound"
in the voices of analyst and analysand is the sound of the
voice of the analytic third "upon their voices crossed." The
analytic third is experienced by analyst and analysand in

the context of the personality system, personal history, sensory awareness, and so on of each individual. As a result, analyst and analysand each speaks with a unique voice; at the same time, each voice is informed by (has an oversound derived from) the unconscious experience in and of the analytic third.

Individuality of voice is not a given; it is an achievement. Uniqueness of voice might be thought of as an individual shape created in the medium of the use of language. This "shape" is one that is made not simply in the medium of language, but in the medium of the *use* of language: voice is an action, not a potential—more verb than noun. The individual voice is not resting dormant, waiting for its moment to be heard. It exists only as an event in motion, being created in the moment. We do not know what our voice will sound like in any situation until we hear it, whether that be in what we say, in what we write, or in what we read aloud. A very large part of what listening to voice entails is the effort to experience, and find words to describe, what the voice in the writing or in speech sounds like, to whom it seems to be addressed, what it is "doing," what effects it is creating, and how it is transforming and being transformed in the acts of speaking, listening, and being heard.

It is misleading to say that voice is "an expression" of the self since this suggests that there is a self "inside" that is speaking through the individual (as a ventriloquist speaks through a dummy), giving audible form to itself. To my mind, it is more accurate to say that voice is an experience of self coming into being in the act of speaking or writing. Speaking or writing becomes a self-reflective experience to the degree that one listens to one's voice and asks oneself, "What do I sound like?" "Who do I sound like?" "How have I come to sound like that?" "Do I want to continue to sound like that?" and so on.

The analysand may never have heard the sound of his own voice before the initial analytic meeting (Ogden 1989a, pp.169–194) and the experience of creating a voice of his own in that meeting (or the feeling that he has been unable to do so) is an experience of enormous importance in an analysis. The analytic setup with its relative absence of visual cues, its unusual rhythm of dialogic give-and-take, and its strong emphasis on the use of language in the service of psychological exploration together powerfully contribute to a greatly heightened sensitivity to the sound tones and rhythms of the analysand's voice.

The analyst, too, is creating a voice for the first time at the beginning of each analysis, and, in a sense, in each analytic meeting. He cannot know before he begins to speak what his voice will sound like and how it will change as he speaks to *this* analysand, in *this* analysis, in *this* analytic hour. As many times as I have entered into an analytic experience with a new patient over the past twenty-five years, I am each time surprised by the fact that I speak with a different voice (more accurately, with a different set of voices in continual transition) with each new patient. I do not—and could not—preconceive the voices with which I hear myself speaking. For me, this is one of the wonders of spending one's life in the practice of psychoanalysis. And it is not only my voice that is different with each patient. When an analysis is going well, my voice and the patient's develop new oversounds in the course of each analytic hour and over the course of the weeks, months, and years that the analysis encompasses.

The surprise that I experience in hearing my voice is often a disconcerting one. There have been times when I have found my voice disappointingly wooden—or cloyingly sweet, or hollowly authoritative, or embarrassingly thin. Voice (my own and the patient's) is always an object of analytic scrutiny, and so even (or perhaps in particular) these disturbing surprises are not unwelcome events, nor are they a source of worry. I am far more concerned by long periods of *absence* of surprise in my experience of my own voice or the patient's. Hearing or feeling stagnation of voice is, for me, one of the experiences on which I rely most heavily to alert me to the fact that an analytic hour or a phase of an analysis has become lifeless. The experience of lifelessness itself, as it is heard and named, is transformed into an event of analytic interest.

4

"The Music of What Happens"
in Poetry and Psychoanalysis

There are the mud-flowers of dialect
And the immortelles of perfect pitch
And that moment when the bird sings very close
To the music of what happens.

S. Heaney, "Song," 1979

In this chapter, I will be asking the reader to do something a little different. I ask the reader to listen to his listening: that is, to listen to the ways he listens, and hears me listening, to a poem; and then to compare those "soundings" to the ways he listens, and hears me listening, to an analytic session. I will try to stay out of the reader's way as he or she does this work, and only at the end of the chapter will I offer some thoughts about what I currently think listening to and saying a poem have to do with listening to and speaking with a patient in analysis.

Before turning to Frost's (1928a) "Acquainted with the Night" and to a session from the twelfth year of an analysis, I will make a few introductory comments. Over the course of the past fifty years, there have been a number of important shifts in the theory and practice of psychoanalysis. Among them is an increasing awareness that the most interesting and productive avenues of analytic inquiry seem no longer to be adequately addressed by the question, "What does that mean?"—that symptom, that set of dream images, that acting out, that rageful response to the sound of the analyst's coughing, and so on. An inquiry into personal meanings has become inseparable from an understanding of the unconscious intersubjective context in which those meanings are generated. Consequently, the question "What does that mean?" has gradually expanded so as to increase greatly the emphasis on such questions as: "What's going on here?" "What's happening between us consciously and unconsciously and how does that relate to other aspects of the patient's (and the analyst's) past and present experience, both real and imagined?" With this shift in our conception of the analytic process comes the need for a commensurate change in the way we use language to speak to ourselves and to our patients. It seems to me that we must develop a capacity to use language in a way that does justice not only to the task of understanding and interpreting the conscious and unconscious meanings of our patients' experience; in addition, our use of language must be equal to the task of capturing and conveying in words a sense of "what's going on here"—in the intrapsychic and intersubjective life of the analysis, the "music of what happens" in the analytic relationship.

In this chapter, I will first look at the ways a poem grapples (often with great success) with the challenge of getting into the language the full richness, complexity, and movement of living human experience. I will not be offering an analytic interpretation of a poem, nor will I attempt to provide a piece of criticism that treats the analytic session as a literary "text." To do so would be to sap the vitality of both the poem and the experience in analysis. Instead, I will address the experience of the Frost poem and the analytic experience each in its own terms. I have made no conscious effort to select a poem that "fits with" or "speaks to" the aspects of human experience that are most alive in the analytic session, or vice versa. I urge the reader to read the Frost poem aloud several times before proceeding to my discussion. Frost's best poems come to life through the play of the sounds and meanings of the words, and the feel of the words in our mouths as we "say the lines" (Frost 1962, p. 911).

While there has been some discussion in the analytic literature concerning aspects of the relationship between poetry and psychoanalysis (see, for example, Edelson 1975; Hutter 1982; Jones 1997; Martin 1983; Meares 1993), as far as I have been able to determine there has been thus far no contribution to either the literary or the analytic literature that undertakes to offer a close reading of a poem and a detailed description of an analytic session, with thoughts about what the two have to do with one another.

I. *"Acquainted with the Night"*

When "Acquainted with the Night" was published in 1928, Frost was in his early fifties and had already achieved extensive recognition as a poet, not only in this country but also in Europe. He and his family, however, were in a state of exhaustion, brought on in large part by Frost's frequent traveling to read and lecture and by the many moves that the family had made (from New Hampshire to England to Massachusetts to Michigan and back again to New England) as Frost pursued his ambition to be not only one of the "great poets," but also a widely read poet. When this poem was written, Frost's wife, Elinor, and their children were in poor health, their daughter Marjorie seriously ill. Frost's third child had died a decade earlier only three days after her birth.

Acquainted with the Night

I have been one acquainted with the night.
I have walked out in rain—and back in rain.
I have outwalked the furthest city light.

I have looked down the saddest city lane.
I have passed by the watchman on his beat
And dropped my eyes, unwilling to explain.

I have stood still and stopped the sound of feet
When far away an interrupted cry
Came over houses from another street,

But not to call me back or say good-by;
And further still at an unearthly height,
One luminary clock against the sky

Proclaimed the time was neither wrong nor right.
I have been one acquainted with the night.

The opening line, an apparently simple sentence, is remarkable for the complexity, subtlety, and self-sufficiency of the language. It is not at all apparent how one should read it. Depending on where the reader places the emphasis in the words "I have been one," a different "sentence-sound" (Frost 1914a, p. 675) is made, each with its own meaning. The line, as I have lived with it and struggled with it, seems to be most enigmatically alive when one says it with equal *lack* of stress on any one of its words. The enormous force of the restraint of this first line is palpable, and it sets the tone for the rest of the poem.

Even the syntax ("the nerve and bone structure of language" [Steiner 1989, p. 159]) of the first sentence contributes to its somber vitality: grammar is pushed to its limit, is unobtrusively broken just a bit, and is newly created. It is as if the structure of language itself is unable to contain "some strange resistance in itself . . . As if regret were in it and were sacred" (to borrow from Frost's [1928b, p. 238] "West-Running Brook"). The "grammatically correct" form of the first line would read: "I am one who has been acquainted with the night." A new grammar (both broken and newly made) is required, which dissolves the immediacy of "I" (or "I am" or "I am one") in the present, and instead creates an unlocalizable past that is present and a present that is somehow already past: "I have been one"—and still am? Or have been until recently? Or used to be, but am uncertain about whether I am now?

The sounds and rhythms of the first six lines of the poem are mesmerizing and inseparable from the connective tissue of the poem's overarching metaphor: the poem as a walk. The poem is not a poem about a walk: the poem *is* a walk. The alternating unstressed and stressed syllables of the iambic meter[1] all but disappear into the larger two-stride "sentence-sounds" of walking-and-breathing-and-thinking-while-walking. The speaking voice naturally breaks the sentences into two parts:

> I have been one [—] acquainted with the night.
> I have walked out in rain—and back in rain.
> I have outwalked [—] the furthest city light.

> I have looked down [—] the saddest city lane.

This "walking poem" (in a style reminiscent of the "walking poems" of Dante and Wordsworth) manages to get into the language what it sounds like and feels like to be alone, talking to oneself in one's head and in one's body (in the sensations and rhythms of breathing and walking and being). The sound of the voice in this poem is not the sound of storytelling or of the narration of experience; it is a sound that is as close as I have encountered in any poem to the background sound of being.

The voice in the first two stanzas manages to encompass not only sadness and loneliness, but also irony and humor—a dark humor—that seem to protect the poem

---

1. Iambic meter is composed of two-syllable units ("feet") in which an unstressed syllable is followed by a stressed one.

and the poet from the embarrassment of excessive earnestness of voice.[2] There is pleasure taken (and perhaps shelter found) in playing with words: "walked out" in line 2 becomes "outwalked" in line 3. The walk is both "in rain" and "reined in." "Looked down" in line 5 carries a double meaning of seeing (experiencing) the sadness in the city lane/line and at the same time the sense of defeating (looking down) the sadness in a battle of I's/eyes locked in struggle (which ends when one or the other turns away, averts his gaze).

Frost seems unable to resist the mischievous use of the phrase "And dropped my eyes" (I's) at the beginning of line 6, the only line in the first two stanzas to begin with a word other than "I." At the same time, this phrase "dropped my eyes" is part of one of the most desolate, and yet thoroughly matter-of-fact, moments in the poem:

> I have passed by the watchman on his beat
> And dropped my eyes, unwilling to explain.

The speaker is not only unwilling to explain, he is unable to explain. The poem itself stands in place of an explanation.

A subtle shift in line 7 is felt largely through the disruption of the sound and rhythm of this walking-

---

2. In a letter to his close friend Louis Untermeyer, Frost (1924) wrote, "Irony is simply a kind of guardedness. So is a twinkle. It keeps the reader from criticism. . . . Humor is the most engaging cowardice. With it myself I have been able to hold some of my enemy in play far out of gunshot" (pp. 702–703).

and-thinking-and-breathing poem: "I have stood still
and stopped the sound of feet." The words "stood still and
stopped the sound of feet" require that the voice pause
after "still" and "stopped" and finally come to a halt mid-
sentence at the end of the line. This stopping of the sound
of feet (both anatomical and metrical) at the end of line
7 is achieved without the help of a period, a semicolon,
or even a comma: for a moment words cease; the rhythm
of walking ceases; the sound of thinking and breathing
cease.

> I have stood still and stopped the sound of feet
> When far away an interrupted cry
> Came over houses from another street,
>
> But not to call me back or say good-by;

Out of the silence comes an interrupted cry, which
has a disturbing, uncompromising otherness to it. It is not
a cry intended for the ears of the speaker, but it is nonetheless a sound that changes him, becomes a part of him,
as it seems to give voice to inarticulate feeling. The word
"interrupted" (both harrowing and utterly indifferent)
is for me the most unexpected and newly made word in
the poem. (What is an interrupted cry?) The sound of
the word "interrupted" itself interrupts the more flowing
phrase that immediately precedes it ("And far away") and
the one that follows ("Came over houses from another
street").

In this part of the poem (lines 7–10), the experience
of being acquainted with the night gathers into itself new

sounds and meaning. The soft rhyming of "night" (in the title and in the first line) and "not" in line 10 ("But not to call me back or say good-by") unobtrusively links the two. Being acquainted with the night is becoming being "acquainted with the not": the "not" of the empty space; the interruption of the cry; the "not" of the force disrupting the rhythm of the poem; the "not" that is the "strange resistance" that will not be reined in by the rules of grammar and the laws of time; the "not" of the "I"/eye that is dropped, and refuses to see or to be seen. But at the same time, the "not" that is being created in this poem is the "not" of imaginative possibility, a space in which something new, something never before heard—the poem itself—comes into being. The not/night of this poem has a reticence about it; the reader will be allowed to glimpse it, hear it fleetingly (in the interruption of the cry and of the rhythm of the words), but the reader will only know/ no it as an acquaintance, never as a friend.

The poem concludes in a surprising way:

And further still at an unearthly height,
One luminary clock against the sky

Proclaimed the time was neither wrong nor right.
I have been one acquainted with the night.

The final four lines of the poem are mystifying, and more than any other part of the poem defy paraphrase. The speaker in these lines seems to marvel at the vast indifference and vast beauty of the night sky. He seems no longer to be asking or expecting that the sounds of the night acknowledge his presence ("to call me back or say good-by"). But at the same time the language is doing something quite different. The poem in these lines personifies, makes human, the "luminary clock against the sky" (a clock tower as metaphor for the moon, or vice versa?) that talks (proclaims) to him (or is it proclaiming to nothing but the night sky?). And what the luminary clock momentously proclaims is the lack of moment—the lack of significance—of the temporal movement, rhythms, and punctuations of life ("the time was neither wrong nor right"). Moreover, the proclamation is delivered not in a hard, mechanical cadence, but in the very human, softly flowing rhythms of Frost's "*living* sounds of speech" (Frost 1915, p. 687).

The "I" that begins the final line is a far different "I" from the "I" that began the poem. It is an "I" that has earned the right to say "I have been one acquainted with the night": I have been one acquainted with the sound of solitary walking-thinking-breathing-being; acquainted with feelings of sadness and remorse and shame that cannot be explained; acquainted with the loneliness and unexpected curiosity stirred by the sound of an interrupted cry; acquainted with the feeling of humility and wonder engendered not only by the indifference of the night, but also by the way that strange inhuman otherness is created in language derived from, and saturated with, the uniquely human living sounds of speech.

All of this, all that the poem is, is unobtrusively gathered together into the sound of the word "night," which is the final sound of the poem. I say final sound and not final word because "night" sets in motion cascading resonances and disruptions of sound (largely through a variety of forms of rhyming) from every part of the poem. In addition to the rhyming of the final word/sound "night" with the "I" that opens the poem (and the six that follow), there are a half-dozen line-ending rhymes with "night," several internal rhymes (by, eyes, neither, time), and a number of soft internal rhymes as well (for example, night/not/nor). These echoes continue to reverberate in the ear long after the final word is said. In this poem of cycles, of endings that are beginnings, there can be no final word.

II. An Analytic Session

From my consulting room I could hear Ms. S, a woman in her late thirties, close the door to the bathroom in my office suite. In the twelve years that we had been working together in a five-session-per-week analysis, it was only in the previous year or so that Ms. S had begun to use the office bathroom occasionally. As I waited for her, I recalled an event that had occurred five or six years earlier: on leaving the bathroom, Ms. S had realized that she had failed to button some of the many buttons on her trousers. In reality, there had been no danger of her pants falling down, but she had experienced intense feelings of embarrassment when she noticed the unfastened buttons. I remembered having suggested to Ms. S that she might have felt that the bathroom was a place where both she and I were undressed (although at different times), and it may have felt as if we had been undressed together in that small room. In retrospect my interpretation seemed heavy handed and formulaic. The "bathroom incident" was followed by several months of profound emotional withdrawal on the part of the patient. At that time, I was practicing at a different office building. I recalled, more in visceral sensation than in visual imagery, what it felt like when the office next to mine was occupied by my closest friend, J, and how empty that building had felt when her office was rented to someone else after her death.

These thoughts and feelings, which began as I heard the bathroom door close, left me feeling diffusely anxious. When I met Ms. S in the waiting room, there was an unexpected and uncomfortable formality about it.

Once in the consulting room and on the couch, Ms. S began without a pause to tell me that she had had a dream the previous night which she was looking forward to telling me. She said that it was an unusual dream in that it was about the two of us and a friend of hers, and not about female students of mine. (For years she had imagined that my students were far more likable and interesting to me than she was.) The dream seemed to her to be a very important one.

> In the dream, your office has very white walls. You have a collection of ten statues in the closet behind your chair. You've had them there all along, but you've never known quite what to do with them. It's you, but you don't look like you. Each of the statues

is a talisman. One represents Victory, and another
Courage. I forget what the others represented. You've
taken them out over the years. My friend, R, is there
and I'm glad that the two of you are meeting one
another. She tells you a story of my swimming in an
ice-covered lake. There is a really nice feeling in listening to her tell you the story. I laugh and say, "I
wouldn't do that now." You take out a statue that has
real green grass growing in it. I think it's a woman
cooking, a woman making things. I forget what happens next, but at the end, R and I leave the office.
In the dream I think that this is my lot in life—I will
have friends, but not a love relationship with a man.
I've begun to accept being alone—I know how difficult I am to be with.

I was struck by the simple directness of the dream.
Things of significance were being taken out of hiding.
Feelings were being accurately named. Her practice of
swimming in an ice-covered lake, which was portrayed
(rather optimistically, I thought) as a thing of the past,
seemed to refer to the patient's chronic state of psychological detachment in which she is unable to know what
she thinks or feels or experiences in her body. Ms. S had
relied heavily in the analysis on histrionic imitations of
feeling, and on efforts to elicit feelings of anger from me
by means of endless provocations. Her ability to get me
angry would momentarily relieve her profound feelings
of psychological deadness. The naming of the statues in
the dream reminded me that the patient's mother, who

was twenty years old when she gave birth to Ms. S, had been so ambivalent about having a baby that she was unable or unwilling to give the patient a name for almost a month after her birth.

After telling me the dream, Ms. S said that she missed the excitement of expecting magic from me each time she came to her sessions. (She was referring to her previously unconscious wishes that "the treatment" would consist of my giving her my thoughts [in fantasy, parts of my vitality and sense of self], which would magically transform her into a person who felt alive—albeit with my feelings.) She told me that in the dream the statues did not feel like magic charms that would give her victory or courage or anything else. They were interesting pieces, particularly the one with the grass growing in it. She said that that statue gave her the feeling that, unlike the other statues in my collection, it was not an object "left over from some ritual performed by an extinct culture"; rather, it felt like it was "part of an event that never stopped happening and is still happening." She said that she had had the thought as she was telling me the dream that I might have been awarded the statues for achievements in my life. But the thing that felt new about the dream was that she did not get stuck, as she often has, in making a story in which she is the outsider trying to steal my life, my achievements, my family, and my friends. She said that in this dream, although there was a sense of being resigned to being alone for the rest of her life, she did at least bring her own friend and her own interests and curiosity.

While the patient was talking to me about her dream, I was feeling quite off-balance, not knowing what to make of what was happening in the hour. Ms. S seemed to be making analytic use of her dream, but it seemed to me quite possible that she was being compliant in coming up with what might have felt to her like "the right answer" (that is, *my* answer) to the dream. I felt that there was a good deal in the dream that I could comment on. For instance, the statue of the woman with grass growing in it might allude to the patient's increasing sense of her own fertility—her own ability to make things with her mind (perhaps even our imaginary baby)—and an enhanced sense of groundedness in her own femininity. This and several other possible interpretations that went through my mind felt flat to me, and I remained silent rather than saying something for the sake of saying it. I found my mind wandering to thoughts about a patient I would be seeing later in the day. That patient had been in a great deal of pain and turmoil at the end of our last session. I felt concerned about her and eager to hear how she was feeling.

Ms. S went on to describe more fully the feeling of hopelessness that she experienced at the end of her dream. She then told me that for several weeks she had been extremely frightened of driving in the rain because she could not see clearly despite the fact that she had twice changed her windshield wiper blades. She had been afraid that she would be killed in a "head-on collision." (This brought to mind the fact that the patient's father, before she was born, had been in a very serious auto accident. He had been chronically depressed before then, but the accident seemed to have exacerbated the depression. From very early on in her life, Ms. S felt that she had served as her father's confidante and [in unconscious fantasy] his therapist, his mother, and his wife.) The morning of the session I am describing, Ms. S's auto mechanic had told her that her windshield had opacified slightly, and needed to be replaced. I began without being aware of it to think about the fact that the older of my two sons, who was living in New York City at that time, would be coming home for a visit in a few days. I was very much looking forward to seeing him, and was going over in my mind the time of his flight, the details of his arrival, and the need to tell him that I would meet him at the baggage claim area. Although for years we had been meeting at the baggage claim area when he came to visit, I felt at that moment in the session a great sense of urgency about reminding him. I felt put upon by him, which seemed odd to me. I realized that my disgruntlement with my son disguised my fear of not finding him or of getting lost. I also realized that the fluorescent airport lighting that I was picturing was associated with a visceral memory of feelings of sadness, emptiness, and fear as I had waited in the airport late one night several years earlier for a flight to New York to visit my father, who was gravely ill and hospitalized.

As I refocused my attention on Ms. S, my partial understanding of the reveries that were occupying me (particularly my irrational annoyance with my older son) led me to be more consciously aware of the sourness and disguised fearfulness that I was experiencing at that moment, and in retrospect had been feeling throughout the session. I think it was my tone of voice more than the content of my interventions that conveyed the emotional change I was undergoing as a consequence of this increased self-awareness.

A little later in the hour, Ms. S said that even though today she was feeling that there was a place for her here in my office, and had even used the office bathroom, she had felt when I met her in the waiting room that I had seemed surprised that it was she who was there. I was quite startled by the simple straightforwardness of her observation. I had the somewhat disturbing feeling that for quite some time in this session, and probably in previous sessions, the patient had been "ahead of me": she was looking forward (through her windshield, and to telling me her dream) while I was looking backwards (to the "bathroom incident" of a half-dozen years earlier, and to the death of a friend). What had previously been for me intellectualized ideas and subliminal feelings and images now began to take on a stark clarity and emotional immediacy. My thoughts and feelings about the trip east to visit my father became an analytic object of a different sort at this juncture. I recalled crossing the street at night in the bitter January cold of New York City with my wife and sons after having visited my father in the hospital. My older son was seventeen at that time, and only a year away from going to college. I had been aware of the intense sadness that I had been feeling about the approach of the time when he would be leaving home, but until that moment in the session with Ms. S, I had not been as fully aware that during that trip east I had been experiencing his leaving as if it were he (and I) who were dying, and not my father.

Although it has required much time and many words to describe this reverie experience, in fact these thoughts, feelings, images, and sensations occupied only a brief period of time. Ms. S went on to say that she had made a decision as she entered my office today not to fold up and put under her head the blanket (which I keep at the foot of the couch) as she had done for the previous month or so: "When I put the blanket on top of the pillow [to remedy back pain], my voice comes from my throat. My voice is fuller and comes from my chest when I don't use the blanket to prop up my head. I wanted to see today what would happen if I didn't use the blanket in that way. As I'm talking about this, I'm so curious about whether you noticed the change. It's only what you think or see or feel that counts. Why do I still need that from you?" This question was followed by a silence of about a minute. I then told the patient that I thought she had been feeling great pride and excitement about hearing the fullness of her voice and the richness of her mind in being able to dream a mysterious and interesting dream and think creatively about it. I added that she had noticed with disappointment that she had interrupted herself as she began to feel that I was the only one in the room who had a mind. Ms. S replied that she had been aware of feeling anxious while telling me earlier in the session that she enjoyed thinking and speaking in a way that felt cre-

ative to her. She said that even though she had been aware
of what she was doing, she could not resist turning to me
in the way that she had. I suggested that she might be
afraid that if she were to feel that she has become a person in her own right, and not simply a carrier of parts of
me, it would mean not only that the analysis would come
to an end, but that we would lose all connection with one
another in an absolute way, almost as if one or the other
of us had died. (I was thinking not only of the feeling in
my reverie that my older son's growing up was equivalent
to his dying and to my feeling utterly lost, but also of the
reverie involving my experience of the absence in my life
[the empty office] following J's death. Also in my mind
was the patient's fear of being killed in a "head-on" collision [a fatal collision perhaps in fantasy resulting from
her having her "head on": that is, from being able to think
and feel her own thoughts and feelings].)

Ms. S cried, and after several minutes said that she
was feeling grateful to me for having talked to her in the
way that I had, and for her ability to talk to me in the way
that she had today. She said that she did not want to say
more because she was afraid of crowding out what she
was feeling with space-filling words.

The patient and I were silent for the final few minutes of the hour. In that time I experienced a quiet feeling of love for Ms. S of a sort that I had never previously
experienced with her. It had a sadness about it. I became
aware in the course of the silence that I felt appreciative
of Ms. S's unconscious effort in this session to teach me
(by showing me) about the struggle in which both of us

were engaged, a struggle to live with the sadness and loss and pride and excitement and sheer inevitability of movement toward separateness that is inherent in growing up and becoming a person in one's own right.

The patient began the following meeting by saying, "I've never met anyone like you before." I laughed, and Ms. S joined me in this laughter. The laughter felt full of affection (and some comic relief) as the two of us looked at ourselves (as if from a distance) after a very long period of strenuously and earnestly toiling with (and at times against) one another. I said, "Maybe you felt that you met me for the first time in yesterday's session. Meeting me in that way is not the same as having a meeting with me."

In the weeks that followed, we talked about the idea/feeling that you can't leave a place you haven't been to. It was only after Ms. S had met me that there could be the possibility of her ever considering leaving me.

III. Discussion

Space does not permit a detailed discussion of the moment-to-moment movement of the analytic process in the clinical material just presented. I will focus primarily on the ways I made use of overlapping states of reverie of analyst and analysand in my effort to "catch the drift" of the unconscious, and to make use of this sense of what was happening to formulate transference interpretations and other interventions.

As discussed in previous chapters, I will use the term "reverie" (Bion 1962) to refer to the daydreams, fantasies, ruminations, bodily sensations, and so on that I view as representing derivatives of the unconscious intersubjective constructions jointly, but asymmetrically, generated by the analytic pair. These intersubjective constructions, which I have called "the analytic third" (Ogden 1994a), are a principal medium in which the unconscious of the analysand is brought to life in the analytic relationship. Almost always, the analyst's reveries seem to him at first to represent mundane and idiosyncratic everyday concerns of his own, having little, if anything, to do with the patient; in fact they regularly feel to him to be distractions and preoccupations ("his own stuff") that reflect how he is *not* being an analyst at that moment: that is, how he is not giving focused attention to what the patient is saying and doing.

The session (and the beginning of the subsequent session) that I presented began when I heard the bathroom door close behind Ms. S. My reverie concerning the "bathroom incident" seems to me in retrospect to have reflected my unconscious wish to view the patient and the analytic relationship as if Ms. S, and my relationship with her, had remained timelessly suspended in that earlier period. The experience of this reverie, which included a sense of the profound absence in my life that resulted from J's death, left me diffusely anxious, and contributed to my feelings of woodenness when I met Ms. S in the waiting room.

The dream that she presented at the beginning of the hour seems, again in retrospect, to have involved a sense of several important changes in Ms. S over the course of analysis: she no longer swims in an ice-covered lake—that is, she no longer lives in a frozen state of autistic encapsulation ("I wouldn't do that now"). She was no longer perpetually engaged in a futile effort to steal life from me parasitically, in order to compensate for her own feelings of deadness. Instead, she had developed to a significant degree a capacity to be fertile, and to make things (the living green grass) that felt real and alive to her. There was also in the dream a feeling that the patient was beginning to consider the end of the analysis (suggested by her leaving me in my office at the end of the dream).

Part of my response to the dream as Ms. S told it was an appreciation of its simple directness. However, although the patient was interested in and curious about her dream, and able to make analytic use of it (for instance, in her comments about no longer feeling single-mindedly intent on getting me to magically transform her), the possible interpretations that occurred to me felt hackneyed and emotionally flat. As I look back on this moment, I seemed to have been anxious about acknowledging that the patient had matured psychologically, and that she was trying to tell me that she was for the first time daring to imagine leaving me (albeit with sadness and disappointment).

As the patient spoke of her feelings about the dream, my own thoughts turned to another patient, one who clearly needed me and who was hardly at all concerned with the eventual termination of her analysis. In this displacement, I was (unconsciously) longing to return to a time in the past when Ms. S had needed and depended on me in a more primitive and desperate way than she did now.

Ms. S's fears about the opacified windshield now seem to me to have reflected her ambivalence about looking ahead. I was unable to hear it at the time, and at that point in the session, I began to ruminate anxiously about meeting my son at the airport, and felt irrationally burdened by having to remind him where we would meet. I also experienced fleetingly (more as a subliminal image than a narrative) a combination of fear, sadness, loneliness, and emptiness as I remembered the night at the airport, waiting for a plane to visit my father when he was very ill.

As my focused attention returned to Ms. S, the combined effect of the reverie experiences that I have described led to an increasing awareness of the anger, sourness, and disgruntlement that I had unconsciously been feeling toward her throughout the session. I also became aware that the anger was serving to protect me against feelings of fearfulness and sadness.

This increased self-awareness and partial understanding was, I think, conveyed to the patient by my tone of voice more than by the content of what I said (my "tone of meaning but without the words" [Frost 1942b, p. 308]). Somewhat later in the session, the patient was able to tell me that I seemed not to have expected to see her when I met her in the waiting room. Her comment startled me, and helped me to consolidate my conscious and subliminal reverie experiences. I became much more fully aware of the way in which I had been unconsciously holding onto the past relationship with the patient while she was (ambivalently) attempting to look forward to her maturity, fertility, and independence. Her observation led to an enrichment of my own reverie experience, and this in turn enhanced my ability to be more fully present with her. I "recalled" a moment of understanding that had occurred years earlier, but nonetheless was in a sense occurring for the first time in this session with Ms. S: the moment of recognition that it was my father, and not my older son or I, who was dying. My son was growing up and leaving home (leaving me), but this was for both of us a form of being alive (albeit full of sadness and feelings of loss as well as pride, excitement, and possibility) and not a form of deadness.

The links between these understandings and what had been occurring in the session with Ms. S now felt palpably real and immediate. Ms. S talked about feeling that she was speaking with a fuller voice having decided not to prop up her head with my blanket (that is, not to use me to prop herself up in a way that made her voice and her sense of self sound and feel thin and insubstantial). However, Ms. S then found herself slipping back into a feeling that she needed parts of me to make up for missing parts of herself.

Speaking from (but not about) my reverie experiences, and in conjunction with the rest of what I understood about what had been happening during the hour,

I spoke with Ms. S at the end of the meeting about her fear that having a mind and a voice and a life of her own would result in so absolute an ending to the relationship with me that it would feel as if one or the other of us had died. The session ended with the patient's expression of gratitude that the two of us had been able to think and talk to one another in the way that we had. Not wanting to supplant a feeling that felt real with space-filling words, Ms. S was silent for the final few minutes of the hour. During that silence I felt a form of love and sadness that I had not previously experienced with her.

In a sense, the session both ended and became the beginning of something new in the opening moments of the following day's session, when Ms. S said, "I've never met anyone like you before." I experienced her comment as both humorous and rich with wonderful ambiguities. After we laughed together, I, without planning to do so, said to her that I thought she must have felt that she had met me for the first time in the previous day's session. I added that meeting me in the way that she had is not the same as having a meeting with me. There had been very little playfulness in the analysis to this point, and so it was a new and welcome experience to both of us to find ourselves taking pleasure in spontaneous play with words and feelings and ideas.

IV. Afterwords

In this final section I will offer some specific comments about what, to my mind and to my ear, the experience of saying, and responding to, "Acquainted with the Night" has to do with the experience of listening to and speaking with Ms. S. Before beginning that discussion, however, I want to make explicit the context for the comparison that I will offer between the uses of language in poetry and in psychoanalysis. A critical divide separates these two pursuits: psychoanalysis is a therapeutic activity, while reading and writing poetry are aesthetic ones. To try to draw one-to-one correspondences between the two represents, I believe, a form of reductionism that obscures and distorts the essence of these two quite different human events.

Analysts attempt (with varying degrees of success) to use language in the service of communicating with the patient in a way that is maximally utilizable by the patient in his (always ambivalent) efforts to achieve emotional growth. Analysts try to achieve aliveness in their use of language in the service of bringing feelings and ideas to life in words that will advance the analytic process. A conscious or unconscious effort on the part of the analyst to be "poetic" in the analytic dialogue (that is, to create beautiful, pithy, artistic forms with words) almost certainly reflects a form of narcissistic countertransference acting-in. Such acting-in will severely impede, if not destroy, the analytic process unless the analyst is able to recognize what he is doing, and subject his thoughts, feelings, bodily sensations, and behavior to analytic scrutiny. The poet, on the other hand, is answerable only to the art that he is attempting to create; *his* failures are lines that lack vitality and imagination, and are devoid of feeling.

In the work with Ms. S, I was attempting to listen and be attentive not only to what she was talking about, but also to the effects created by the way she and I were using language. This way of attending to language determined to a large degree the forms and qualities of my ways of being and talking with her: that is, my "analytic technique"—a very dry name for a very lively thing. In the session described I did *not* "translate" into "unconscious terms" what Ms. S was saying with an interpretation like: "Your feeling at the end of the dream of being resigned to spending the rest of your life without a love relationship with a man represents your unconscious disappointment and anger about the fact that you feel that you and I will never have a romantic relationship." I am aware that this imaginary interpretation is heavy handed, but I am illustrating what I believe to be a flawed interpretive posture which excessively treats the patient's words and sentences, images and ideas, as symbols to be seen through and presented to the patient.[3] Such an approach to the language of interpretation (either of a poem or of analytic experience) presupposes that feelings and ideas are there, "behind" the repression barrier "in the unconscious," waiting to be mined (brought to mind) and ex-

---

3. Searles (1959) has observed: "Surely many a neurotic patient in analysis . . . finds himself maddened on frequent occasions by his analyst's readiness to discount the significance of the patient's conscious feelings and attitudes and to react to preconscious or unconscious communications as if these emanated from the only 'real' and 'genuine' desires and attitudes" (pp. 282–283).

posed to the light of day—that is, brought into the light of conscious attention and secondary process thinking. When I speak of "translating" or "decoding" symbols, I am referring to a rather mechanical form of listening to patients: one that assumes a unidirectional movement—from symbol to symbolized, manifest to latent, conscious to unconscious—as opposed to a form of listening that is responsive to the rich reverberations of sound and multilayered meanings that lie at the heart of both poetry and psychoanalysis. Of course, all interpretation of verbal symbols and the emotional context in which they are created involves, in one form or another, a search for a meaning/content that is unspoken and perhaps unspeakable. In this sense, all interpretive listening involves to some degree "listening through" the language. I am suggesting, however, that interpretation becomes dryly explanatory ("this means that") when the emphasis on the "listening through language" is too great. Moreover, I believe that the unspoken and the unspeakable are present (sometimes in their absence) in the language that *is* spoken, in the manner in which it is spoken, in the sounds of the words and sentences, in the feelings elicited in the listener, and (in the analytic setting) in the behavior and bodily sensations that accompany what is being said.

In the analytic session presented, I made use of a set of reveries that at first were only subliminally available to me (more sensation than thought). I treated my reveries neither as distractions from the "real" work of analysis nor as packets of pure unconscious meaning. Rather, I treated them (to the degree that I could achieve and maintain awareness of them) as an indirect (associational) method of talking to myself about what was occurring unconsciously between Ms. S and me. This way of approaching the experience of reverie reflects a perspective from which the unconscious is not imagined to reside *behind* the reveries or at the end of a chain of reverie associations, but as coming to life in the movement of feeling, thought, imagery, and language of the reverie experience itself.

At some point it becomes necessary that the analyst recast his reveries into a more highly organized, verbally symbolized form of talking to himself (and eventually to the patient) about the affective meaning of the reverie experience, as it pertains to and is derived from what is going on at an unconscious level in the transference-countertransference. This act of bringing one's experience into a verbally symbolized form is not a necessary part of saying poems. At times, a reader may find it useful and interesting to try to talk to himself about what is going on in the language of a poem (as I have done in my discussion of Frost's poem), but the reader of a poem may at other times prefer to let the poem remain a predominantly sensory experience that need not, and perhaps cannot, be transformed into a verbally symbolized response. In fact, the impossibility of doing justice to a poem in one's efforts to paraphrase it reflects something of what distinguishes poetry from other imaginative uses of words (for example, in novels and in short stories where plot and character development carry far greater significance than they do in lyric poetry).

Toward the end of the session with Ms. S, on the basis of my (always tentative) understanding of my reverie experience, I said to her that I thought that at that moment growing up felt both dangerous and exciting to her. It seemed that the independence involved in being an adult felt to her as if it necessarily brought with it the end of all connection with me, a disruption that felt as absolute as the death of one or the other of us. In saying this, I was not telling Ms. S what she *really* felt, or what lay under or in back of what she thought she felt. Rather, I was making use of metaphoric language in an effort to draw one aspect of her experience into relation to another in a way that created something new: a way of seeing and experiencing herself that had not previously existed.[4]

As my listening to Ms. S did not primarily involve an effort to get "behind" what she was saying, my way of listening to the Frost poem was not most fundamentally an act of "translating" or "decoding" symbols. For example, I was approaching the poem in a way that does recognize that the night at times seems to represent the darkness of despair, and at other times seems to represent the mysteriousness of the vast otherness that surrounds us and of which we are a part. But in the reading

---

4. Metaphor (in contrast to the "decoding" of the unconscious meanings of symbols) inherently creates an unfilled space of possibilities between the two elements, which are being drawn into a relationship of similarity and difference—not one of equivalence.

I presented of "Acquainted with the Night," I was primarily engaged in an effort to listen to the sound and feel of what the language was doing as I said the lines. For example, in the final four lines of the poem, the language gracefully—celestially—keeps turning in on itself in a way that seems to have no end. Even as the speaker seems to be marveling at the vast nonhuman otherness of the night sky, the language is doing something quite different in personifying (making human) the "luminary clock against the sky" that speaks (proclaims) the arbitrariness of time while the language of the proclamation (the poem itself) is alive with the very human, very beautiful rhythms and cadences of "the *living* sounds of speech." The beauty and mystery of the human and the nonhuman weave in and out of one another like the sides of a Möbius strip.

It seems to me that one of the most fundamental similarities between Frost's "Acquainted with the Night" and the fragment of the analysis of Ms. S is the way each achieves its emotional force through what Frost called "feats of association" (quoted in Pritchard 1994, p. 9). In other words, both the poem and the analytic session generate both powerful resonances and powerful cacophonies of sound and meaning. I have discussed how, in the Frost poem, the final word/sound "night" gathers into itself, through resonances of sound and sense all that the poem is, all of its exquisitely beautiful sounds and all of its aridity, all of its flowing, ethereal parts ("One luminary clock against the sky") and all of its disrupted parts where the ear "stands still" in sadness and in wonder when "an interrupted cry / Came over houses from another street."[5]

Ms. S's comment, "I've never met anyone like you before," is no less alive in its associative richness than is the interrupted cry in the Frost poem. Her statement set in motion remarkable feats of conscious and unconscious association, which in very many ways drew upon what was most alive in the current moment and in the preceding session and made of all of it something new through her use of language. (See Boyer 1988 for a discussion of the relationship between unresolved transference-countertransference feelings in one analytic session and the opening moments of the next one.)

---

5. The juxtaposition in this paragraph of my experience with Ms. S and my experience with the Frost poem underscores for me another difference between analytic and poetic experience. The former (in this case) involves a relationship of a dozen years in which millions upon millions of events (in psychological and external reality) occurred (for example, experiences of many grades of intimacy and distance, of anger and love, of hopefulness and immense frustration). An experience with this poem, even though it is a poem that I value greatly, cannot possibly capture the range and depth of experience of a twelve-year relationship. I think that perhaps this difference in the experiences explains in part why my responses to the poem tended to center more on the universal elements of experience (which are made immediate and personal by the poem), while the focus of my analytic attention tended to be on what was most specific and unique to my experience with *this* patient in *this* analytic hour.

Italo Calvino (1986) has commented that the rhyming of words in poetry has an equivalent in prose narrative where "there are events that rhyme" (p. 35). I would add that in the analytic setting there are conscious and unconscious feelings, thoughts, and other intrapsychic and intersubjective events, that rhyme—"that echo each other" (p. 35). For example, Ms. S's word/idea/sound "met" had lively connection with ("rhymed with") her observation (in the previous session) that when I met her in the waiting room, she felt that it was not she whom I expected to meet. Ms. S's dream involved a "meeting": a friend of hers (perhaps an aspect of herself) met me for the first time and made a comment; this caused the patient to laugh in a good-natured way that feels to me closely associated with the laughter at the beginning of the following session. In addition, Ms. S's comment about meeting me held an important resonance with still another "meeting": the imaginary one with my son, in which he and I would be meeting at the airport as if we had never met there before. These reverberations were not sequential but instantaneous, and they generated a comically poignant moment in which both Ms. S and I experienced an intensified sense of being present together, but as separate people, in that moment.

This "rhyming" of the word/idea "met" in these different forms of the experience of meeting made for a rich and lively ambiguity and expressiveness. Ms. S's highly compact statement suggested that she was meeting me in the sense of seeing me (knowing me as a separate person) for the first time; that she was meeting me in the sense of being equal to me (able to meet the force of my presence); that she was meeting me in the sense of making a rendezvous with me, perhaps a romantic meeting. Her comment conveyed in an instant all of these feelings/ meanings and more.[6]

The sound of Ms. S's voice assured that the "like you" in "I've never met anyone like you before" conveyed tender feelings of fondness for me (of "liking me") and not simply a comparison of me with all the other people she had met.

And then there is the word "be," unobtrusively tucked into "before," bringing the experience of being to the fore. Ms. S was in an important sense bringing herself into being as she developed a voice of her own with which to speak.

In short, I have rarely received a more loving and interesting gift than the one Ms. S gave me wrapped in the words "I've never met anyone like you before."

---

6. These "feats of association" related to (actual and fantasied) meetings and partings give renewed vitality to the concept of "over-determination" (Freud 1900, p. 283), revealing it to be more verb than noun, and to have as much reference to the future as it does to the past. In the analytic fragment under discussion, it seems to me useful to view overdetermination as a process in which meanings and feeling tones come into being and accrue in such a way that the experiential outcome cannot be foreseen and is forever in motion: "like giants we are always hurling experience in front of us to pave the future with" (Frost 1939, p. 777). The overdetermined, from this perspective, always has a good deal of the "yet to be determined" about it.

Perhaps what is most fundamental to both poetry and psychoanalysis is the effort to enlarge the breadth and depth of what we are able to experience. It seems to me that both poetry and psychoanalysis at their best use language in a way that encompasses a full range of human experience—as Jarrell (1955), speaking of Frost, put it—from "the most awful and the most nearly unbearable parts to the most tender, subtle, and loving parts, a distance so great" (p. 62). Both poetry and psychoanalysis endeavor to "include, connect, and make humanly understandable or humanly ununderstandable *so much*" (p. 62).

The movement of sound and cadence of loneliness and sadness and possibility in "Acquainted with the Night," and the movement of feelings of anger, fear, sadness, disappointment, and love in the session with Ms. S, represent efforts to generate experiences in which two people (poet and reader, analyst and analysand) may become more fully capable of living with, of remaining alive to, the full range and complexity of human experience. These efforts are made even in the face of "humanly understandable" and "humanly ununderstandable" conscious and unconscious wishes to evacuate, pervert, subvert, or in other ways kill the pain of being humanly alive. Perhaps the almost irresistible impulse to kill the pain, and in so doing kill a part of ourselves, is what is most human about us. We turn to poetry and to psychoanalysis in part with the hope of reclaiming—or perhaps experiencing for the first time—forms of human aliveness that we have foreclosed for ourselves.

5

Borges and the
Art of Mourning

Every poem, in time, becomes an elegy.
J. L. Borges, "Possession of Yesterday," 1982

And now Borges—for him the entire universe is in every one of its particles; all of literature in every book ever written and yet to be written. This book of conversations at the frontier of dreaming would be sorely lacking without the sound of Borges's voice.

In this chapter, I attempt to learn about mourning as it comes to life in the conversation between Jorge Luis Borges, the man of letters, and Borges, the man *in* letters—the speaker/character/voice in his writing. In particular, I will be exploring the idea that mourning is not simply a form of psychological work; it is a process centrally involving the experience of *making* something, creating something adequate to the experience of loss. What is "made," and the experience of making it—which together might be thought of as "the art of mourning"—represent the individual's effort to meet, to be equal to, to do justice to, the fullness and complexity of his or her

117

relationship to what has been lost, and to the experience of loss itself.

The creativity involved in the art of mourning need not be the highly developed creativity of the talented artist. The notion of creativity, as I conceive of it here, applies equally to "ordinary creativity," that is, to the creativity of everyday life. What one "makes" in the process of mourning—whether it be a thought, a feeling, a gesture, a perception, a poem, a response to a poem, or a conversation—is far less important than the experience of making it.

I will discuss two of Borges's writings: "Pierre Menard, Author of the *Quixote*" (1941), and "Borges and I" (1957). The particular significance of these works in relation to the experience of mourning derives in part from a set of internal and external circumstances in Borges's life that surrounded the writing of these fictions/prose poems. Both pieces were written at critical junctures in Borges's life, each involving experiences of enormous loss. As one would expect, a musician will mourn by making music, a painter will mourn in the act of painting, an analyst in engaging in an analytic relationship or perhaps in writing about (and from) his or her analytic experiences. Borges mourned in the act of writing poems. It is the experience of mourning brought to life in these two prose poems that will be the principal subject of this chapter.

The structure of this chapter is a rather loose one, intentionally. There are three sections (a biographical sketch and discussions of the two Borges prose poems);

each is of interest to me in its own right, independent of its connection to the experience of mourning. No life, and no poem, addresses itself to a single facet of human experience: every aspect of one's life, every feeling state generated in a lived experience or in a successful piece of writing, is integrally connected with every other aspect of life and every other feeling state.

In the brief biographical sketch that begins the chapter, I will treat the events of Borges's life not as a way of "explaining" his writing from a psychoanalytic perspective, but as a set of experiences that stands in conversation with his writing. To a very large degree, the biography of a writer is to be found in the author's writing: the life of a writer is, in a sense, the life of his writing. The experience of writing is the place where a writer is most alive; it is the place where he lives. I will, with only a few exceptions, leave it to the reader to listen for, and do with what he or she will, the resonances between the life of the man and the life of the writing. In this way, we as readers are not only eavesdroppers on, but also participants in, the "conversation" between the life and the work.

In the second part of the chapter, I will discuss Borges's fiction, "Pierre Menard, Author of the *Quixote*" (1941) in an effort to listen to the ways Borges uses language within the structure of the literary genre that he invented early in a period of profound mourning. That literary form, as Borges developed it over time, would come to influence significantly the development not only of twentieth-century Latin American and Spanish literature, but of Western literature as a whole.

In the final section, I will discuss the prose poem, "Borges and I" (1957), which was also written near the beginning of a period of great loss for Borges, the repercussions of which would powerfully color the last three decades of his life. The sound and structure of mourning in "Borges and I" and in "Pierre Menard" are quite different. As he had done fifteen years earlier in "Pierre Menard," Borges in "Borges and I" creates a literary form in which to bring to life (and bring to death) a particular experience of mourning.

Borges: A Man of Letters

From his birth in 1899, and perhaps even before his birth, circumstances conspired to bring Borges into a family whose emotional life seemed to be structured in large part by a schism regarding language itself. Borges's parents, as did many young couples in turn-of-the-century Buenos Aires, lived with his paternal grandmother (his grandfather had died some years earlier). This rather banal matter of social custom, driven by economic expediency, set the stage for a fateful family division. Borges's paternal grandmother, born and raised in Staffordshire, England, had married an Argentine and lived the rest of her life in Buenos Aires. Her son, Borges's father, grew up speaking English with his mother, whose strongly Anglophilic temperament led her to make only modest efforts to achieve fluency in Spanish. From very early on, Borges's grandmother read stories to him in English. As he grew, Borges read widely from the almost exclusively English language books in his father's extensive library: "If I were asked to name the chief event in my life, I should say my father's library. In fact, I sometimes think I have never strayed outside of that library" (Borges 1970, p. 209).

Borges's mother came from an Argentine family with a long and distinguished military history. The house in which he grew up was something of a family "military museum" (Rodriguez Monegal 1978, p. 6), where photographs, uniforms, swords, and other military objects were displayed that attested to the valor, courage, and dignity of Borges's maternal forebears. These silent men of action and stalwart, devoted women had little interest in literature.

Not surprisingly, given this family constellation, Borges learned to read English before he could read Spanish. Borges, in fact, was so thoroughly bilingual that for a period of time in childhood he recalls not knowing that he was speaking two different languages. It felt to him that he was speaking a single language that took different forms depending on the circumstances (Guibert 1973, p. 81).[1] For Borges, what he later learned to be the English language was the form of language he spoke with his father and paternal grandmother—the language of stories and ideas, the language of the books in his father's library. Spanish was the form of language he used when speaking of the events of everyday life—the language he spoke with

---

1. It must be kept in mind that Borges's "recollections" are stories told by one of the great storytellers of the twentieth century, a man who wrote reviews of nonexistent books by imaginary authors.

his mother and her parents as well as with servants. Borges (1970) recounts that having first read *Don Quixote* in English, "When later I read *Don Quixote* in the original, it sounded like a bad translation to me" (p. 209).[2]

It is impossible to overestimate the depth of Borges's love and admiration for his father: "My father was very intelligent, and like all intelligent men, very kind. . . . It was he who revealed the power of poetry to me—the fact that words are not only a means of communication but also magic symbols and music" (Borges 1970, pp. 206–7). Borges's father aspired to be a writer, and managed to complete a novel along with several other books and a

---

2. The English that Borges heard in the stories his grandmother read him and in the books he read from his father's library was nineteenth-century literary English. Recent translations of Borges's writing from Spanish to English (Hurley's translation of Borges's [1998] fictions, for example) have attempted to create a style of English that corresponds to the twentieth-century Buenos Aires Spanish that Borges used in his poetry and fictions. These translators believe that earlier translations of Borges's work into English (for example, di Giovanni's translations, in which Borges very actively collaborated) used a formal, "old-fashioned" style of English (Rodriguez Monegal 1978) that fails to capture Borges's Spanish writing style and voice. To my mind, this is as it should be; Borges's English was nineteenth-century literary English, not twentieth-century spoken English. This was the English that Borges spoke when he lectured to English speaking audiences (as in his Harvard University lecture series *This Craft of Verse* [*1967–1968*], recently released on compact discs). Consequently, I have elected to use an earlier translation of Borges by Donald Yates and James Irby (1962) as the text for my discussions of Borges's literature.

series of poems; none of these were ever published. "From the time I was a boy, when blindness came to him [Borges's father], it was tacitly understood that I was to fulfill the literary destiny that circumstances had denied my father. This was something that was taken for granted (such things are far more important than things that are merely said)" (Borges 1970, p. 211). Characteristic of Borges, that final parenthetical aside, delivered with such nonchalance, is the most lively and telling part of what is otherwise a rather unremarkable account of a son's wish/burden to attempt to fulfill his father's dreams.

Though the Borges family employed servants, they were a middle-class household living in the Palermo district of Buenos Aires, at that time one of the shabby outskirts of the city. It was a district in which middle- and working-class families lived (with a moderate sense of danger) in close quarters with hoodlums and prostitutes. Aside from the hours passed in his father's library, most of Borges's time as a child was spent in the garden at the rear of the house, where he and his younger sister, Norah, would invent games. There were no other children in Borges's early life, in part because his father and grandmother insisted that he be educated at home until he was more fully formed (which turned out to be the age of nine).

Along with his father and his grandmother (and three generations before her), Borges was born with a congenital malformation of his eyes, which results in impaired vision from birth, and leads to a progressive deterioration of sight until total blindness is reached in middle age. (Borges's father lost his sight completely not long after he turned forty).

His impaired eyesight, along with his rather frail constitution, rendered Borges utterly unsuited to a military life.

> As most of my people had been soldiers—even my father's brother had been a naval officer—and I knew I would never be, I felt ashamed, quite early, to be a bookish kind of person and not a man of action. . . . I did not feel I deserved any particular love, and I remember my birthdays filled me with shame, because everyone heaped gifts on me when I thought that I had done nothing to deserve them— that I was a kind of fake. After the age of thirty or so, I got over the feeling. (Borges 1970, pp. 208–209)

Borges's depiction of himself as a youth unexpectedly takes on a darkly humorous tone in the final sentence, as he "slips in" the fact that what had sounded like feelings restricted to childhood were, in fact, a sense of himself that required decades, not months or years, to overcome. In truth, he never did completely overcome these feelings, which in adult life took the form of revulsion for his body (Rodriguez Monegal 1978, pp. 348–349). Borges no doubt included himself when he wrote wryly of an early nineteenth-century Argentine writer, "Like all men, he was given bad times in which to live" (1946, p. 218).

Borges was something of a child prodigy. At the age of nine he published in a prestigious Buenos Aires literary magazine a Spanish translation of an Oscar Wilde story. "Since it was signed merely 'Jorge Borges,' people naturally assumed the translation was my father's [Jorge Guillermo Borges, a lawyer and teacher of psychology and English]" (Borges 1970, p. 211). From very early in his childhood, Borges's sense of his own worth was inseparable from his sense of himself as a reader, writer, and thinker.

Despite the fact that by the age of thirty, Borges had published three volumes of poetry as well as a large number of essays on philosophical and literary topics, he was still a relatively unknown poet and literary figure even in Buenos Aires. Borges paid for the publication of three hundred copies of his first volume of poems, which he gave away to friends and slipped into the pockets of coats in the cloakroom of a major Buenos Aires magazine publisher. About that volume of poetry, *Fervor de Buenos Aires* (1923), Borges late in his life commented with his usual entanglement of sincerity and self-parody, "I feel that all during my lifetime I have been rewriting that one book" (1970, p. 225).

Unable to earn a living as a contributor of articles to newspapers and literary magazines, Borges, who was still living at home at thirty-six, took a position as an assistant librarian in a small regional branch of the municipal library. His nine years there were lonely and extremely unhappy ones, filled with a profound sense of futility. As there was virtually no work for the library staff to do, Borges spent his days hidden among the uncatalogued stacks of books writing poetry and essays.

In February 1938, Borges's father died. Borges is un-
usually silent in interviews, and in his autobiographical
essay (1970), about the meaning that that event held for
him. He says only that there was a sense of relief associated
with his father's death, as it brought an end to physical
suffering that had gone on much too long. Perhaps the
most telling commentary on his father's death is Borges's
linking of that event with another event that same year:
"It was on Christmas Eve of 1938—the same year my
father died—that I had a severe accident" (Borges 1970,
p. 242). On that Christmas Eve, Borges had arranged to
introduce to his mother a young woman he was very fond
of. That morning, rushing up the staircase of the library
in which he worked, he accidentally cut his head on the
edge of a recently painted casement window that had
been left open to dry. Borges's poor eyesight probably
contributed to not having seen that the window had been
left open. The wound became infected and led to a septi-
cemia, very high fevers, hallucinations, and loss of the
capacity to speak. For almost two weeks it was unclear
whether he would survive.

On recovering from the illness, Borges was terrified
that it had left him unable to read or write or think imaginatively. To demonstrate to himself that these capacities
had not been lost or impaired, he set himself the task of
writing "something I had never really done before. . . . I
decided I would try to write a story. The result was 'Pierre
Menard, Author of the *Quixote*'" (Borges 1970, p. 243).

As is characteristic of Borges, there is both overstatement and understatement in his account of this critical

juncture of his life. In fact, he had published one fictional story five years earlier, "The Street Corner Man" (1933)—which he later said was so bad that it was an embarrassment to him. He also had published, in an established literary magazine, the book reviews I mentioned earlier, of nonexistent books by nonexistent authors. At first these were successful hoaxes, but over time they became simply a form in which Borges liked to write. So writing fiction was not entirely new to Borges in 1938. The overstated element of Borges's account, however, is dwarfed by the dimensions of the understatement: Borges, in trying "something I had never really done before," was in fact trying something *nobody* had ever really done before. He had set himself the task of creating a new literary genre—one that would bear his unique signature.

It is difficult to define the essential qualities of the literary genre created by Borges. His *ficciones* ("fictions"), as he called them, were short pieces, usually about four to eight pages in length, having in common with poetry an extreme compactness and self-sufficiency of language, as well as a highly refined sensitivity to the sound and rhythm of words and sentences. When they succeed, they earn the name "prose poems."[3] Their language is so dis-

---

3. In the foreword to a collection of his poems (including several prose poems), Borges (1971) wrote, "I suspect that poetry differs from prose not, as many have claimed, through their dissimilar word patterns, but by the fact that each is read in a different way. A passage read as though addressed to reason is prose; read as though addressed to the imagination, it might be poetry. I cannot say

tilled that a single word or phrase or parenthetical aside may convey what other writers require a lengthy paragraph or a chapter to achieve.

Borges's fictions almost always involve an encounter with, or a discovery of, someone or something "fantastic"—that is, something discontinuous with ordinary waking life, as if dream-life had subtly, unobtrusively insinuated itself into a corner of waking life (or vice versa). Like lyric poetry, Borges's fictions are virtually without plot; they are also without developed characters, save for the voice of the speaker.[4] The speaker is both the author, Borges (the real person writing the fiction), and a character in the fiction. It is here that Borges's fictions are most enigmatically, paradoxically, and energetically alive and most continually at play: the character/speaker is the invention of the author, while at the same time the author is brought to life (created) in the writing through the voice of the speaker/character. The storytelling, not the story or the symbolism, is the real literary event in these fictions.

---

whether my work is poetry or not; I can only say that my appeal is to the imagination" (p. xv). Some years later, he added, "Good prose must be poetry" (1984, pp. 52–53). For these reasons, I use the term "poetry" to refer to Borges's fictions (when the writing is good). Viking recently published a selection of Borges's poems (1999), and a collection of his fictions (1998); many of the pieces included in the collection of fictions appear also among the selected poems.

4. What Borges said of the characters (the ciphers) in Dante's *Inferno* is equally true of the characters in his fictions: "They live in a word, in a gesture; they need do nothing more (Borges 1984, p. 15).

The intricate structure of the writing in Borges's fictions is perhaps what is most remarkable and most distinctive about them: they have the structure of an endless labyrinth with no center and no exit; the labyrinth and the universe become indistinguishable from each other, as do dreaming and waking life, imagination and reality, character and writer.

Borges's manuscripts, despite his failing eyesight, were invariably written in meticulous, tiny handwriting that seems to reflect the delicate structure of his writing. The manuscripts, with their seemingly endless crossed-out words and sentences, bear witness to the extraordinary number of revisions that each fiction underwent as he pared away every unnecessary word in his attempts to achieve irreducible essences.

Borges, Author of "Pierre Menard, Author of the Quixote"

In the years immediately following the death of his father and "the accident," Borges entered a period of enormous creativity as he developed and refined the genre that he called "fictions." His fictions were collected in two volumes, *Ficciones*, published in 1944, and *El Aleph*, published in 1949, and are considered by literary critics, and by Borges himself, to be his "two major works" (Borges 1970, p. 244). These years following his father's death were not only a period of great literary achievement, they were also years of intense loneliness. In a piece written in 1940, but not published until 1973, Borges presented a fictional account of his own suicide. (There is no evidence to suggest that Borges was suicidal during this period.)

It was in this emotional context that Borges (1941) composed the first of his fictions, "Pierre Menard, Author of the *Quixote*." This work moves at a dizzying pace: in the space of the two opening sentences, the story establishes its form as a mock essay written to rectify a fallacious and diminishing cataloguing of the work of the recently deceased fictional novelist Pierre Menard. The speaker/Borges, having examined Menard's "personal files" in a feverish effort to correct this indignity, provides a meticulous listing (lettered "a" through "s") of Menard's complete "visible work." Among the nineteen writings listed (none of which is a novel) is item "e": "A technical article on the possibility of improving the game of chess, eliminating one of the rook's pawns. Menard proposes, recommends, discusses and finally rejects this innovation" (Borges 1941, p. 37). Other entries include: "An examination of the essential metric laws of French prose, illustrated with examples taken from Saint-Simon (*Revue des langues romanes*, Montpellier, October 1909)" (p. 37); and "A manuscript list of verses which owe their efficacy to their punctuation" (p. 38).

There is a sadly comic quality to the "rectified" catalogue. The list feels strained in its self-conscious cleverness, and generates a sense of the flatness of "the remains" of a deceased writer. It has something of the maudlin sobriety of a mortician's handing "the effects of the deceased" to the grieving family.

After the meticulous, chronological, utterly absurd listing of Menard's complete "visible" work, "Pierre Menard" takes a surprising turn. The shift is not so much a shift in plot (because there is no plot); the transformation is achieved largely by a change in voice: from the almost maniacal passion of the first part of the "essay" to the awe-struck, reverential tones of the second part. Even in its awe, the speaking voice is never without an ironic edge. There is "other work" to be introduced, and *this* is "the subterranean, the interminably heroic, the peerless" (p. 38) work of Menard.

Borges, through a series of letters written to him by Menard, learned of Menard's attempt at a literary feat so daunting that it is doubtful that anyone had ever before conceived of such an undertaking, much less tried to carry it out. Menard had set himself the task of writing the *Quixote*, not a pointless manual transcription of Cervantes's *Quixote*, or additional chapters for the *Quixote*, or even a modern version of *Don Quixote*. He had set out to write the *Quixote* itself. "The first method he conceived was relatively simple. Know Spanish well, recover the Catholic faith, fight against the Moors or the Turk, forget the history of Europe between the years 1602 and 1918, *be* Miguel de Cervantes. Pierre Menard studied this procedure (I know he attained a fairly accurate command of seventeenth-century Spanish) but discarded it as too easy" (p. 40). His writing here has all the speed and density and luminosity of the poetry of Dante or Blake, but would never for a moment be mistaken for their work because of the sad, ironic edge that undercuts the feeling-tone of every sentence, be it one of bravado or humor or charm. How could one achieve, in a form other than the one devised by Borges, the effects created by the list of impossible preliminary tasks that ends with an un-expected, sweep-of-the-hand, two-word dismissal of the plan to become Cervantes as "too easy"?

Borges follows with an aside (a favorite form of his, in which he seems to step out of the fiction into "real-ity"—which turns out to be only another fiction). In this aside, Borges addresses the reader's inevitable response to Menard's brazen claim that becoming Cervantes is too easy a method of writing the *Quixote*: "Rather as im-possible! my reader will say. Granted, but the undertak-ing was impossible from the very beginning and of all the impossible ways of carrying it out, this was the least interesting" (p. 40). These words are spoken with a sense that the logic underlying the statement is irresist-ible, inevitable: if one is going to go to all the effort of attempting the impossible, of course one would adopt the most interesting (even if the most difficult) of all the impossible methods one could imagine. To *be* Cervantes and arrive at the *Quixote* through him would be pointless, even if one achieved it: that feat has already been accomplished by Cervantes. Why do it again? The great difficulty and the great significance of Menard's attempt to write the *Quixote* lie in the fact that he would achieve it through his own experience as a man of the twentieth century. There is, at the same time, "a certain melancholy" (to borrow Borges's words from the opening paragraph of the fiction) asso-ciated with the idea of Menard's/Borges's (the two are gradually becoming one) devoting the major effort of his literary life to finding his own way into a text already written.

Menard and Borges vacillate as to whether the task Menard had set for himself was impossible or merely "almost impossible" (p. 41). Menard concedes, "I should only have to be immortal to carry it out" (p. 40); but a page later he reasons that his task of writing the *Quixote* was no more difficult than that faced by Cervantes before he had written it: "my general recollection of the *Quixote*, simplified by forgetfulness and indifference, can well equal the imprecise and prior image of a book not yet written" (p. 41).

The fiction seems to be preparing itself and the reader for its most decentering moment, which occurs when Borges juxtaposes a passage from Cervantes's *Quixote* and the same passage from Menard's *Quixote*:

> It is a revelation to compare Menard's *Don Quixote* with Cervantes'. The latter, for example, wrote (part one, chapter nine):
>
>> ... truth, whose mother is history, rival of time, depository of deeds, witness of the past, exemplar and adviser to the present, and the future's counselor. . . .
>
> Menard, on the other hand, writes:
>
>> ... truth, whose mother is history, rival of time, depository of deeds, witness of the past, exemplar and adviser to the present, and the future's counselor. (p. 43)

The reader cannot resist moving back and forth between the two passages—only to discover that the two are identical, word for word, comma for comma. In so doing, the reader finds that he has become a character in the story, bearing witness to the fact that Menard did indeed succeed in writing a portion of the *Quixote.* More important, the reader must attest to the fact that the experience of reading Menard's *Quixote* is an experience altogether different from reading Cervantes's *Quixote,* and far more interesting: "(More ambiguous, his detractors will say, but ambiguity is richness.)" (p. 42). The experience of reading the passage written by Cervantes is an experience of wonder at the beauty of the sound of the words and the grace with which phrases and ideas are poured one into the next, creating in the language the feeling of sounds and ideas coming into being, each giving birth to the next.

Menard's "version" creates quite a different effect and generates a radically different set of meanings: "History, the *mother* of truth: the idea is astounding. Menard, a contemporary of William James, does not define history as an inquiry into reality but as its origin. Historical truth, for him, is not what has happened; it is what we judge to have happened" (p. 43).

Menard, a twentieth-century "novelist," invests the seventeenth-century narrator of the *Quixote* with a twentieth-century pragmatist sensibility and casts twentieth-century ideas in seventeenth-century language. What is "astounding" about Menard's version is that the movement of this metaphoric "flow" of phrases and ideas is not

only a movement forward from the past to the present
to the future. It is at the same time a movement backward
against itself as the past is created by the present. The
invasion of the seventeenth century by the twentieth, and
vice versa, is not simply anachronistic; rather, it creates
its own idiosyncratic experience of time. Borges knew
from his own childhood experience the imaginative possibilities, as well as the impossible entanglements, that are
created when one interfuses the language and literature
and spirit of twentieth-century Spanish and nineteenth-
century English "(perhaps without wanting to)" (p. 44).

What is most alive about this fiction is not the magic
of the "fantastic" undertaking and the partial (but extraordinary) success of Pierre Menard in writing the
Quixote; something far more important to Borges is being
addressed. We begin to sense subliminally, as the two ver-
sions of the *Quixote* are juxtaposed, that Menard's writing
of the *Quixote* is a wonderful metaphor, not for writing,
but for reading: a metaphor for "good reading," a type
of reading that invents the writing, that invents the
Quixote, that invents the seventeenth century, and that
invents the fiction we are reading.

Borges is interested in (more accurately, consumed
by) how one generation of writers (and readers) in-
fluences/creates another:

> Some nights past, while leafing through chapter XXVI
> [of the *Quixote*]—never essayed by him [Menard]—I
> recognized our friend's [Menard's] style and something
> of his voice in this exceptional phrase: "the river nymphs

and the dolorous and humid Echo." This happy conjunction of a spiritual and a physical adjective brought to my
mind a verse by Shakespeare which we [Menard and
Borges] discussed one afternoon:

Where a malignant and a turbaned Turk. . . . (p. 40)

In this passage, Borges is subtly suggesting that the
sound of Menard's writing voice can be heard in Cervantes' style and voice, and that the voices of Menard and
Cervantes, (and Borges) can be heard in Shakespeare's
style and voice (and Shakespeare's voice in theirs).

"Pierre Menard" is an extraordinary experience in
"ear training" (Pritchard 1994), which succeeds as few
other pieces of writing do as an unselfconscious lesson
in reading. This fiction manages to convey a visceral
awareness that language has a life of its own. Menard's
language and Shakespeare's and Cervantes's and Borges's
(four different tongues spanning four centuries) are
nonetheless one language that is nobody's possession—
they (and we) each borrow it, and use it, and it uses us,
for a time.

Immediately after Borges's stunning juxtaposition of
the passages from the *Quixotes* of Menard and of Cervantes,
something jarring happens in the writing. Beginning with
the sentence, "There is no exercise of the intellect which
is not, in the final analysis, useless" (Borges 1941, p. 43),
the identity of the speaker becomes ambiguous. In this
way, the language continues to meld Menard the character, Borges the character, and Borges the writer. This sen-

tence and those that follow have a nihilistic shrillness that is quite absent in the playfulness of the first two "sections" of this fiction—the parody of academics picking at the bones of a recently deceased author and the account of Menard's maniacal/heroic (quixotic) effort to write the *Quixote.* These tones give way in the final paragraphs to a resigned acknowledgment that applies equally to Menard, to Borges the speaker, and to Borges the author:

> . . . he set himself to an undertaking which was exceedingly complex and, from the very beginning, futile. He dedicated his scruples and his sleepless nights to repeating an already extant book in an alien tongue. He multiplied draft upon draft, revised tenaciously and tore up thousands of manuscript pages. (pp. 43–44)

In a footnote (a pedantic, self-parodying structure) attached to the end of these sentences, Borges recalls Menard's "quadricular notebooks, his black crossed-out passages, his peculiar typographical symbols and his insect-like handwriting." He also remembers Menard's solitary afternoon walks around the outskirts of Nîmes, where he would "make a merry bonfire" of those notebooks (p. 44 n.1).

It is impossible to read these lines without being reminded that for Borges, to write in Spanish was to write in a second literary language—second to the English language of the stories that his grandmother read to him and second to the English language of the books in his father's library, outside of which he sometimes felt he "never strayed" (Borges 1970, p. 209). Further, the "already extant book" that Menard/Borges aspired to write cannot be separated in the mind of the reader from Borges's desire/need to write the books "already extant" in his father's unfulfilled literary aspirations. There is a great poignancy to this footnote, which creates, for the first time in the fiction, images and a language for Menard's/ Borges's loneliness and profound sense of futility. We are reminded of Borges's own endless revisions in his own tiny handwriting, which in these sentences are rendered nonhuman and more than a little bizarre and repellent by the adjective "insect-like."

Immediately after the footnote Borges (1941) adds: "He did not let anyone examine these drafts and took care they should not survive him. In vain have I tried to reconstruct them" (p. 44). At no other point in this fiction is the finality of death so starkly confronted. There is an absolute end to writing—an end to a life that even Borges (the character, the writer, the man) and his conceptions of circular time cannot undo or "reconstruct" (p. 44).

The fiction continues: "Thinking, analyzing, inventing (he also wrote me) are not anomalous acts; they are the normal respiration of the intelligence" (p. 44). As is his habit, Borges is writing about the experience of writing and reading: thinking, inventing, reading, and writing imaginatively are rather ordinary, very human, highly essential events—the "normal respiration" of our thoughts and feelings and imagination, including the ways we go about grieving for what we cannot achieve for ourselves and for others, and for what we have lost and cannot "reconstruct" (p. 44).

The final paragraph of the fiction begins: "Menard (perhaps without wanting to) has enriched, by means of a new technique, the halting and rudimentary art of reading: this new technique is that of the deliberate anachronism and the erroneous attribution" (p. 44). Borges is describing (rather plainly) the literary genre that he is in the process of inventing even as we are reading these lines. The sound of this sentence is not the sound of the recognition of an enormous achievement (an achievement of the impossible!). It is an unassuming, quietly elegant statement about the achievement of good reading (and secondarily, of good writing). With its simple and lovely phrase—"the halting and rudimentary art of reading"—this sentence has the feel of Borges writing with genuine humility his own epitaph (and that of his father and grandmother). It is an epitaph for those who have enriched, not primarily the art of writing, for that has a life of its own, but the art of reading.

Borges and "Borges and I"

In 1938, the year of Borges's father's death and "the accident," Borges's poetry and essays were popular among the literati of Buenos Aires, but virtually unknown outside of that city. The fictions that Borges wrote over the ensuing fifteen years were well-received and gradually established Borges's literary reputation—not only among readers of Buenos Aires's literary magazines, but among a general readership throughout Argentina.[5] As his reputation as a writer was growing, his vision was deteriorating. Borges's doctors warned him in the late 1940s that if he continued to read and write, the loss of his remaining sight would accelerate. (Of course, he ignored their warnings—what else could he do?) But by 1955, his blindness had reached the point where he could no longer read and write.

In roughly the same period in which Borges's fictions were being published (1939 through 1955), Borges found to his surprise that he had become a symbol of Argentine opposition to the Perón regime. This occurred partly as a consequence of his publication of allegorical poems and essays celebrating civil resistance to earlier dictatorships in Argentina. With the overthrow of the Perón government in 1955, Borges was appointed director of the National Library in Buenos Aires, which at that time contained more than 800,000 volumes. In his "Poem of the Gifts" (1960a), Borges writes of a "God, who with such splendid irony / granted me / books and blindness at one touch" (p. 117).

After 1955, Borges found that he was no longer able to write his fictions; their highly distilled sentences and delicate structures, involving innumerable reworkings and endless "crossed-out passages . . . in his insect-like

---

5. It was not until 1961, when he shared with Samuel Beckett the first Fomentor Prize, that Borges achieved international recognition.

handwriting" required his being able to see the words and sentences on the page. He could compose only by dictating, to anyone who was willing to be his scribe. His writing was limited to shorter prose poems of a far less tightly woven structure than the earlier fictions, and to metrical verse (as opposed to his earlier free verse). Borges found that he was better able to retain these literary forms in his memory while composing.

"Borges and I," published originally in 1957, is a prose poem—quoted here in its entirety—that Borges composed not long after he had lost his ability to read and write:

> The other one, the one called Borges, is the one things happen to. I walk through the streets of Buenos Aires and stop for a moment, perhaps mechanically now, to look at the arch of an entrance hall and the grillwork on the gate; I know of Borges from the mail and see his name on a list of professors or in a biographical dictionary. I like hourglasses, maps, eighteenth-century typography, the taste of coffee and the prose of Stevenson; he shares these preferences, but in a vain way that turns them into the attributes of an actor. It would be an exaggeration to say that ours is a hostile relationship; I live, let myself go on living, so that Borges may contrive his literature, and this literature justifies me. It is no effort for me to confess that he has achieved some valid pages, but those pages cannot save me, perhaps because what is good belongs to no one, not even to him, but rather to the language and to tradition. Besides, I am destined to perish, definitively, and

only some instant of myself can survive in him. Little by little, I am giving over everything to him, though I am quite aware of his perverse custom of falsifying and magnifying things. Spinoza knew that all things long to persist in their being; the stone eternally wants to be a stone and the tiger a tiger. I shall remain in Borges, not in myself (if it is true that I am someone), but I recognize myself less in his books than in many others or in the laborious strumming of a guitar. Years ago I tried to free myself from him and went from the mythologies of the suburbs[6] to the games with time and infinity, but those games belong to Borges now and I shall have to imagine other things. Thus my life is a flight and I lose everything and everything belongs to oblivion, or to him.

I do not know which of us has written this page.

The opening line of the poem feels like an invitation to the reader to enter a labyrinth; the open space behind is still visible if we turn to look, but we do not look back because there is something compelling, almost mesmerizing, going on in the forward movement of the deceptively simple language:

The other one, the one called Borges, is the one things happen to.

---

6. "Suburbs" is a poor translation of the Spanish word *arrabal,* which in this line refers to the shabby outskirts of Buenos Aires where Borges grew up and about which he wrote innumerable poems and stories (my footnote).

There is a doleful sound to these words, generated in part by the series of concessions that the language is making. "The other one" is given pride of place, as it stands alone in the opening phrase of the poem. "The other one" is not only seen but "called," a pun pointing both to the sense of being sought (called after) and having a "calling," a force that affords direction and a sense of purpose. "The other one" is called "Borges," a name that he shares with the author but apparently not with the speaker. (Only a few words into the opening sentence, divisions of divisions of self are taking place like an endless elaboration of forking paths.)

That "the other one" shares a name with the author creates in the language a writer as character, alongside (or is it within? or identical to?) the author as "flesh-and-bone" person who lives in a place "not found in verse" (Borges 1960b, p. 131). The reader is by this time fully within the poem as labyrinth where the words serve as a guide "who only has at heart your getting lost" (Frost 1947, p. 341).

The final phrase of the opening sentence further names "the other one" as "the one things happen to." What would it mean to be someone to whom things do not happen? Is that what it means to cease coming into being, or to be no one, or to not be?

The voice of the opening sentence has a sadness conveyed by the continual negation of the speaker—the one not called, who has no calling, who has no name (not even the pronoun "I"), who lacks even sufficient substance to be a self-as-object ("me") who might become "visible" as a consequence of things happening to one-self. And yet something else is happening at the same time in this elegantly simple, highly compact sentence—something so delicate and subtle that it is hardly noticeable. Despite the multilayered negation of the speaker, it is the speaker, and not "Borges," who has a voice and consequently the potential to bring himself into being in this poem through his use of language. "The other one, the one called Borges" is mute, disconnected from the act of speaking:

> I walk through the streets of Buenos Aires and stop for
> a moment, perhaps mechanically now, to look at the arch
> of an entrance hall and the grillwork on the gate; I know
> of Borges from the mail and see his name on a list of
> professors or in a biographical dictionary.

The "I" of this second sentence is a weak "I," who aimlessly walks the streets of Buenos Aires and stops "perhaps mechanically now." An important dimension of the language here and throughout the poem is the continuous tension between the negation of "I" (here an aimless and at times mechanical "I") and the immediacy of the voice speaking not only in the present tense, but in the present moment—"now." The speaker seems to be addressing neither the reader nor even himself in a meditative way; rather, there is a feeling that the speaker has innumerable times gone over this ground, both in the literal sense of endlessly walking the streets of Buenos Aires and in the metaphorical sense of ruminatively repeating these thoughts, with no expectation of achieving a fresh idea or feeling.

As is the case in the opening sentence, and as is true of virtually every other sentence of this poem, this second sentence is a divided one. In its second half, the speaker explains that what he knows of "the one called Borges" he knows through written words: his name on letters received in the mail, on a list of professors, in an entry in a biographical dictionary. While the speaker lives in the present—the present tense of "I know" and "[I] see"—"Borges" is a part of the past. The letters written to him, the list of professors, the entry in the biographical dictionary are all writing that was done at some previous point in time.

The speaker's voice becomes far more personal as he lists the things he "likes":

> I like hourglasses, maps, eighteenth-century typography, the taste of coffee and the prose of Stevenson; he shares these preferences, but in a vain way that turns them into the attributes of an actor.

Almost twenty years after "Pierre Menard," the list with all its density, its tension between the sequential and the simultaneous, the myriad felt but unstated linkages among its elements, is still a favorite structure for Borges. The list of things that "I like" ("like" is such an unpresuming verb) has wholeness and integrity only in relation to the person who made it—and that person is, in a sense, composed in the process of "making" the list. The "list" seems to draw together, in fewer than fifteen words, the essential being of the speaker. Hourglasses make time visible to one who can see, and audible and palpable to one who cannot. They are the embodiment of the consecutive nature of time: each grain is piled on top of the ones preceding it like corpses dropped into a mass grave. But with a turn of the wrist, time becomes circular—the corpses of one moment become the newborns of the next, softly, quietly elbowing each other in their jostling for entry into the world from within the body of time.[7]

Second only to hourglasses on "the list" are maps. Maps do with space what hourglasses do with time: streets, cities, countries, planets, galaxies are transformed into markings on paper that can be held and felt in one's hands and seen, if one can see, in a single glance. Thus, in the space of two words, all time and space are "captured"—not in sand and glass and paper and ink, but in words used metaphorically. Certainly the words comprising this list are "not only a means of a communication but also magic symbols and music" (Borges 1970, pp. 206–207). In a sense, the elements making up the list and the list making up the speaker (and the writer) are fundamentally metaphors for the imaginative making of

---

7. From very early on, Borges must have been painfully aware (unconsciously, if not consciously) of the relentless progression of time, measured by the progressive loss of his vision. It is difficult to imagine that he did not see himself in the future in the unforgiving, irreversible descent into blindness that he was witnessing in his father and grandmother.

metaphors and for the act of bringing oneself into being through the imaginative use of language.

The feeling in the voice of the poem shifts in the space between the two halves of this sentence. The things liked (and likened), tumbling over one another in the list that comprises the first half of the sentence, give way to the sound of a voice not often heard in Borges's work. It is a voice that feels naked, stripped of irony and wit. The juxtaposition of the two halves of this sentence creates a sense of giving and taking away. The serenely beautiful words of the first half of the sentence, each selected with care—"hourglasses, maps, eighteenth-century typography, the taste of coffee and the prose of Stevenson"—are scorched by the aridity and barrenness of the language of the second half: "he shares these preferences, but in a vain way that turns them into the attributes of an actor." These are abstract, textureless words ("vain" and "the attributes of an actor") that feel more spit out than spoken. The soft, simple words "I like" become the stiff, formal clause "he shares these preferences" in the second half of the sentence.

The tone of the poem as a whole undergoes a powerful shift in the caesura in the middle of this sentence. There is a sense of things unraveling, spiraling downward, in what follows:

> It would be an exaggeration to say that ours is a hostile relationship; I live, let myself go on living, so that Borges may contrive his literature, and this literature justifies me.

The words and clauses of this sentence have the sound and cadence of the thud of body blows being delivered solidly, unrelentingly. This is achieved through the cumulative heaviness of the phrases "I live," "I let myself go on living," "so that Borges may contrive his literature," "and this literature justifies me." (The stiff, moralistic, and legalistic word "justifies" has a chilling deadness to it.)

> It is no effort for me to confess that he has achieved some valid pages, but those pages cannot save me, perhaps because what is good belongs to no one, not even to him, but rather to the language and to tradition.

The idea that language "belongs to no one" plays a role in one way or another in almost all of Borges's poems, fictions, and essays. The idea is not original to Borges, of course, but is brought to life freshly every time he makes use of it (when his writing is good). For instance, the excitement of "discovering" this idea, as if for the first time, in "Pierre Menard" stands in contrast with its use in "Borges and I," where it becomes a club with which to beat down "Borges's" illusions of originality.

The speaker's combativeness and bitterness (which pose at times as even-handedness) are transformed into something subtly new in the succeeding sentence:

> Besides, I am destined to perish, definitively, and only some instant of myself can survive in him.

There is an undisguised sadness and resignation in these words. The speaker, who had earlier been speaking in and for the present ("now"), is a voice becoming the past (concerned not with life, but with afterlife— a writer's survival in his literature after his death). To survive in "Borges," "the other one," is not to survive as a person living in the present. "Borges" is a stolid monument that "survives" not in the sense of living and changing and becoming, but in the sense of commemorating the writer he used to be and the writing he used to make.

As the speaker goes on to talk about Spinoza's notion that "all things long to persist in their being; the stone eternally wants to be a stone and the tiger a tiger," the reader can hear the unspoken final clause of the thought: "And the writer longs to persist in his being as a writer." From this point onward (and backward to the beginning), the poem delves more and more deeply into the experience of the speaker/author struggling (at times unsuccessfully) to persist in his being as a writer.

> I shall remain in Borges, not in myself (if it is true that I am someone), but I recognize myself less in his books than in many others or in the laborious strumming of a guitar.

No simple division between "Borges," the public figure, and Borges, the private, everyday man, is adequate to what is going on in this poem. "Borges" is not simply a construction of the literary world, nor is he a construction (a mask, a persona) invented by Borges, the man. Rather, "Borges" is Borges, who is no longer Borges: no longer the writer recognizable to himself in the writing that has earned him a modicum of fame.

If the speaker is to become someone, if Borges is to become Borges, he will have to achieve it in his writing, in the writing of this poem, "now," in the ever-insistent, almost mocking, present tense of this poem. If he is to become someone, it will not be by recreating the writing of Borges, the author of *Ficciones*, for that Borges is gone, memorialized in biographical dictionaries and in the memory of the speaker (and of the reader). The loss of Borges is almost annihilating, almost beyond comprehension, almost beyond grief. The struggle embedded in the sound of the words and in the torn structure of the sentences of this poem is the struggle to find a way to grieve when there may be nothing left of oneself with which to grieve (when one genuinely does not know "if it is true that I am someone"). "Borges and I" is, in this sense, an elegy arising not from the experience of grief but from the effort to come into being as a writer by arriving at the feeling of grief through the experience of writing. The poem is an elegy for Borges (who is "Borges"), the imaginative writer who once took such pleasure in playing with the structure of language in the writing of his fictions.

That the work of mourning is achieved, or at least begun, in "Borges and I" is felt by the reader in the final line of the poem:

I do not know which of us has written this page.

This is no mere literary trick; it comes as a genuine surprise, a surprise that remakes itself freshly each time I read this poem. Up to its closing sentence, the poem is structured as a series of intoning declarative statements of "I": "I walk," "I know," "I like," "I live," "I am destined," "I am giving over," "I am quite aware," "I shall remain," "I recognize," "I tried," "I shall have to imagine," "I lose." And then finally, like a pyramid balanced on its pinnacle, the edifice of the poem concentrates itself into a second paragraph of less than a single line, beginning with the words "I do not know."

The final line surprises as it does because the speaking voice, the "I" of the sentence, is a new and remarkable event. It is an event that could not have taken place until this moment, a sound that could not have been made in the absence of the work and the art of mourning that precede it. The final line speaks with the voice of an "I" who can speak for "us"—for Borges and "I"— for the first time. There is something at the same time triumphant and sadly accepting in this final statement of not knowing. The triumph of the line and the success of the poem as a whole lie in the paradox it creates: In order for a writer to address his experience of no longer being able to write in the way he had once been able to, he must write an elegy that imaginatively, enigmatically, musically achieves in its language something adequate to all that has been lost. An elegy, this elegy, does not begin with grief; it is an effort to achieve grief in the experience of writing. An elegy, unlike a eulogy, must take in and be equal to (which is not to say identical to) the full complexity of the life that has been lost. The language of a poem that is an elegy must be enlivened by the loss or death of the person or aspect of oneself who is no longer.

In other words, an elegy, if it is to succeed as "Borges and I" succeeds, must capture in itself not the voice that has been lost, but a voice brought to life in the experiencing of that loss—a voice enlivened by the experience of mourning. The new voice cannot replace the old ones and does not attempt to do so; no voice, no person, no aspect of one's life can replace another. But there can be a sense that the new voice has somehow been there all along in the old ones—as a child is somehow an immanence in his ancestors, and is brought to life both through their lives and through their deaths.

6

Re-Minding the Body

There is little in the practice of psychoanalysis more per-
plexing (or more interesting) to me than the question of
how experiences in analysis facilitate the healthy development of the patient's sense of being alive in his or her body.
In health, the experience of being bodied and the experience of being minded are inseparable qualities of the
unitary experience of being alive. Achieving this kind of
sense of aliveness is particularly problematic when early
childhood experience (whether precipitated by constitu-
tional hypersensitivity, inadequate maternal provision, or
trauma) has led the individual to create a pathological
form of mindedness that is disconnected from experiences in the body. Under such circumstances, thinking
tends to be anxiously preoccupied with the achievement
of absolute self-sufficiency: in the realms of both bodily
sensations and internal and external object relations
(Gaddini 1987; McDougall 1974; Tustin 1986; Winnicott

1949, 1952). This goal is pursued by hypertrophied mental activity designed to anticipate, understand, explain,
measure, create, and annihilate (and in all these ways
omnipotently control) everything that happens in the
experience of the body, as well as in relationships to external and internal objects. This sort of defensive mental
activity feels disconnected from the body: sensations stem-
ming from the body so threaten to overwhelm the individual that not only his sanity, but his very being, are felt
to be under siege.

The analysis of a patient who had been both ne-
glected and traumatized in early childhood helped me
to gather impressions that had been accruing over the
course of many years of analytic work. In the fragment of
the analysis that I will present, the important interventions were not preplanned. In fact, they came as a surprise to me, and I find them particularly interesting and
in need of scrutiny for that reason. I had in these instances
a sense of "I-ness" (a feeling of who I was in that moment
with that patient) that was reflected as much in the sound
of my voice (which was for me a very sensory experience)
as in the content of what I said. This "I-ness" was not entirely known to me before I heard it in my voice and felt
it in my body. It was a voice highly personal to me, and at
the same time unmistakably the product of the shared
unconscious experience generated by the patient and me
in the course of the analysis.

Integrally connected with this sense of "I-ness,"
which was brought to life in the medium of voice, was a
form of intervention that also felt new to me, although

not discontinuous with my ongoing experience of who I am as an analyst. In the period of analysis that I will discuss, I found myself telling the patient an imaginary present-day story (based on the patient's history and the history of the analysis). This story, and the patient's experience of my telling it to him, served to make available to him symbols and a human connection with me that he could use to project himself and me into the past. In this way, he succeeded in humanizing what had been for him an inhumane, solitary, inarticulate, unthinkable set of psychological and bodily events.

Clinical Illustration:
A Man with His Back to the Wall

Mr. S, a highly successful thirty-eight-year-old attorney, consulted me because he felt he was fading away as a person, and—even more disturbing to him—he increasingly did not seem to care. Over a period of years he had felt himself gradually withdrawing from his family, his work, and his colleagues. As the analysis proceeded, it became clear that such feelings of withdrawal were by no means new; they had permeated his life from as far back as he could remember. Mr. S held himself responsible for the failure of his previous marriage and for the problems in his current one. He described himself as "constitutionally incapable" of ever admitting he is wrong. This "blind stubbornness" prevented the healing of any rift in a relationship, so the discord in virtually every relationship he had eventually became so severe as to lead to its demise.

Since my interest in this chapter is in exploring a sequence of interventions and responses that took place in the fourth year of Mr. S's analysis, I will offer only a schematic overview of the analytic events leading to the sessions I will discuss here. During the first years of our work together, the analytic relationship was marked by intensely charged efforts on the part of Mr. S to engage me in intellectual "jousting." He would take a "devil's advocate" position on virtually any topic, doggedly defending one side or the other of a complex matter. (Which side of the argument he adopted seemed arbitrary—it was the experience of arguing that mattered.) In this period of our work, the patient and I in the transference-countertransference relied heavily on the largely unconscious defensive fantasy that feats of the intellect (in "combat" situations) had the power to protect him (and me) from painfully out-of-control bodily sensations, as well as from the terrifying aspects of internal and external reality that threatened to overwhelm him (and me). This work led Mr. S and me to view his aggressive "stubbornness" as representing (at least in part) an unconscious attempt to maintain his sanity in the face of what felt like impending psychic fragmentation.

As the work progressed, Mr. S fearfully and ashamedly told me (in bits and pieces that were both confused and confusing) about a series of sexual molestations that he had experienced in his childhood. These molestations had occurred over a period of two or three years, beginning when Mr. S was three or four. Since he had never told anyone about them as they were occurring, he did

not know for sure how old he was at the time, or how long
they went on. His feeling/belief that the molestation
had in fact occurred was based on fragmentary but vivid
memories of the experience, and on a very brief discussion many years later with his older brother. In this conversation, Mr. S learned that his brother had been
molested by the same man, a next-door neighbor, in a
virtually identical way. The patient remembered the
neighbor, a "family friend," taking him into a garage,
backing him into a corner, and fondling his genitals.

Prior to the analysis, the patient had never spoken
with anyone (including himself) in any depth about the
molestation. Neither he nor his brother had told their
parents or anyone else about the molestation as it was
going on; their "conversation" with one another about it
(which occurred some twenty years after the fact) consisted of only a few sentences. Mr. S said that he hated
the idea of making a big deal of it, or of being viewed (or
viewing himself) as a victim: "The current fashion of
everyone's being the victim of child molestation disgusts
me." He tried to treat the molestation as "water under
the bridge." The sad defensiveness of this posture became
evident to Mr. S over the course of the analysis, particularly as he became able to experience the enormous
shame he felt over the fact that he had felt sexual excitement (along with feelings of numbness, terror, unreal-
ity, and confusion) during the molestation. Mr. S and I
came over time to view his combative "stubbornness" as
an unconscious effort to maintain his sanity in the face
of real and imagined threats to his life, beginning in early

childhood. From this vantage point, his "stubbornness" came to be understood paradoxically as one of the healthiest aspects of his personality, reflecting as it did an unwillingness to submit, to lose himself, or to be crushed by another person's will.

Mr. S's father was a very successful international financier who spent almost all of his time traveling in connection with his business. The patient's mother was a depressed, passive woman who stayed at home "with the children," although she rarely played with them or even spoke to them except in operational ways: "It's time for dinner"; "Don't stay up too late"; "Be sure to brush your teeth." When the patient was two or three, his mother began drinking heavily, and taking tranquilizers prescribed by the family doctor. In one of the sessions leading up to the one in which I made two significant unplanned interventions, Mr. S talked about having spent a great deal of his childhood trying to cheer his mother up by anticipating her needs (for example, by getting her cigarettes or coffee) or by trying to think of ways that he could help her to feel better. "There was always in the background the threat that she would kill herself."

The patient's life as a child (when he was not attending to his mother) was, to a large degree, a life of endless story-making and daydreams, into which he retreated. This state of mind, which served as a substitute for life in the external world and in his body, was unpredictably disrupted by the neighbor's molestation and by the demands posed by his mother's depressed moods and implicit suicidal threats.

With the foregoing very brief overview of the initial years of Mr. S's analysis in mind, I will now turn to a series of sessions that occurred during the fourth year of Mr. S's analysis. In the first of these, I was quieter than usual. Mr. S said, "I can't find you today." The patient was remarkably sensitive to the ebb and flow of my emotional presence during his sessions. It was true that during the initial part of that meeting I had been feeling extremely drowsy and had been fighting off sleep. I said to Mr. S that his description of his efforts, day after day, year after year, to keep his mother alive must have been exhausting. (Being with Mr. S that day had been terribly draining for me, but I did not say that to him since that would have made my psychological state the most important event of the hour, thus replicating the patient's early relationship with his mother. Neither did I say that he was experiencing me as distant and self-absorbed, just as he had experienced his mother. To have done so would have further confused the patient by treating his perception as a projection.) I told Mr. S that I thought I had sought a place to rest during the session—something Mr. S could not afford to do as a child, feeling as he did that his mother's life was in his hands.

Later in that session I said to Mr. S that I thought that he might have stood out as a target for sexual abuse because of what the neighbor knew about his family, or might have discerned of the patient's feeling of having no internal or external adult presence to protect him. His parents were for him nowhere to be found, as I had been earlier in the hour. I was aware even as I was making this intervention that it felt contrived, even though there may have been some truth to the idea. It seemed to me that I was trying too hard to demonstrate that I was knowledgeable about the circumstances in which child molestation occurs. Mr. S responded to my comment by saying that he guessed that he felt that way as a child, although it was so much a part of life for him that he never would have thought to describe it in that way.

In the next session, Mr. S told me a dream that consisted of a single image: "There was a tall tree that felt menacing. It might even have been able to talk." He connected the feeling in the dream with a feeling he thought he must have had as a child about the "enormous height" of the neighbor compared to his own height. Of course, it occurred to me that the big, ominous tree may have represented not only the large physical and emotional presence of the neighbor, but also his penis. At this moment in the analysis, I decided to stay at the level of the patient's more conscious experience in order not to violate his privacy by seeming to be able to read his mind.

As the patient was telling me his dream, I was reminded that I had been "coincidentally" filled with sadness the previous evening by a set of lines (accompanied by names and dates) drawn on the wall of a bedroom closet in my home. These markings were a record of the increasing heights of my two sons as they grew up. That evening I had been amazed that the earliest marking was only a foot and a half or two feet from the floor. That lowest line had been drawn when my younger son was only ten months old. It was not the fact that nineteen years had elapsed since the line had been drawn that had so moved me; it was the thought of the utter dependence of that very small child who had needed me to help him stand with his back to the wall so that he could have "his line" drawn. This reverie had a strong sensory component to it and I could feel, almost as a present event, the soft skin of my son's arms and torso as I helped him stand. I said to Mr. S, in response to his dream and my reverie, that when he was molested, he wasn't much taller than the low table near the analytic couch. (Though I was speaking *from* my reverie experience, I was not speaking *about* it [Ogden 1994a, 1997a, b].)

With all this in mind (and in bodily sensation) I met the patient in the waiting room the following day for our session. He seemed unsettled as he walked into my office and lay down on the couch. He began immediately by saying that he was angry with everybody. He was furious with a "dimwit" driver of a car who had stopped in the middle of an intersection and caused a traffic jam. The driver had seemed not to know whether to drive forward or backward, and had "just sat there doing nothing."

It seemed apparent that Mr. S unconsciously (and perhaps to some extent consciously) was experiencing both himself and me as maddeningly ineffectual. I decided not to offer that perception as an interpretation because it seemed to me that the effect of an interpretation (an act of defensive "knowing" on my part) would

have undercut his feeling that I was an impotent, ineffectual analyst and he an ineffectual person. It seemed
better for both of us to live with these feelings for a while
without trying to dispel them. I found myself thinking
about a discussion I had had with a friend about the
Internet, in which I had said that I felt that there was such
a thing as having too much information. I then recalled
not wanting to be told the sex of our second child after
the amniocentesis had been performed on my wife. Our
first child was a boy, and even though I had no strong wish
that the new baby be a girl, I was looking forward to the
experience of making room in myself to be the father of
a girl, at least for the duration of the pregnancy. That was
an experience that I continue to value highly, since the
baby was a boy and I will never again have a daughter of
my own as I did for those months. Although it has taken
quite a lot of words to describe the movement of emo-
tion in this reverie, these thoughts occupied only a few
moments of "real time."

    After the patient had gone on at some length about
a list of grievances he had with various people, and after
I had experienced and been affected by my own reveries
involving both fears of knowing too much and the experience of knowing more (after the amniocentesis) by
knowing less, something changed. The interpretation
that had seemed premature and defensive a few minutes
earlier, now in a modified and far more specific form,
seemed apt. I said to Mr. S that he had mentioned in the
past that he felt that I put pressure on him to experience

feelings associated both with the molestation and with the sense he had as a child of being utterly on his own. He had said that to experience these feelings made him feel terrified and out of control. I added that he might be feeling angry at me today for putting him in that position once again. (Only after saying this did I become aware that my choice of words alluded not only to a psychological position, but also to a submissive bodily position.)

Mr. S was silent for a minute or so and then began moving about on the couch in a very agitated way, rolling to one side of the couch and then to the other as if trying to find relief from physical pain, but failing to do so. He told me that he was afraid that he was going crazy and would never recover. He did not know how he could possibly work in this state of mind, and it seemed certain to him that he would lose his job as a result. During the preceding year, the patient had become similarly disorganized and agitated during two or three of our sessions, but the agitation and confusion this time was by far the most intense and prolonged of these experiences. I said to him that I thought that he was experiencing something of what it must have felt like when he was a small boy being molested—a feeling of losing his ability to think and to control his body, of losing all sense of who he is. Mr. S sat up on the edge of the couch and put his head in his hands. He said to himself out loud, "That's a window, that's a plant, that's a rug" (clearly attempting to hold on to external reality).

When he again told me pleadingly that he was terrified that he would never recover from this feeling of going crazy, I spontaneously said to him, "I won't let that happen." I meant this when I said it, although I was aware that I was promising a lot. Mr. S quieted a little and lay back down on the couch trembling. I kept talking to him so that he would know I was there. I said to Mr. S, "Imagine what it would be like if you, at your present age, were taken without warning into a corner and had your genitals fondled by a man who was as big as a tree. And you would have every reason to believe that this would happen unexpectedly at any time again and again for the rest of your life. And you wouldn't be allowed to tell anybody about it ever. That's more than any boy or any man can possibly take in or live with." (I was aware that I was using the experience of the sexual molestation as a symbol for a large conglomeration of experiences of neglect and overstimulation that Mr. S had experienced both during and between the episodes of molestation, and in his "privileged" role as his mother's guardian and confidant.)

The patient's body, which had been contorted and twisted on the couch, now visibly relaxed. He said that his head felt calm and his body felt "wired . . . no, that's not the right word . . . it feels jazzed."

I said, "It is as if what was going on in your head has been downloaded into your body." He laughed with delight and said, "Yes, but in downloading it, it changed. It feels like something entirely different from what had been in my head. My body feels tingly. . . . no, that's not it either. It's just that I feel my body's being there. I almost never feel that I have a body. It's a curious feeling, I like it." Later that day he left a phone message saying that he felt better and that he felt very grateful to me.

Mr. S began the next session by saying that as he walked to my office he thought that what he'd like to do is lie down on my couch and sleep. He then said that this wish felt connected with a dream that he had had the previous night. "In the dream I was supposed to analyze a baby. I wasn't sure what that meant or how I would go about doing it. I walked into the baby's room and saw the baby sleeping in his crib. I lay down on a bed next to the crib and we slept. Then a man came in. He looked like the pediatrician I had as a kid. I liked him but even though it looked like him I knew it was you. He just watched the baby and me sleeping for a while and then he left."

I said to Mr. S that he had told me how as a child he was continually trying to figure out ways to make his mother feel better and to get his parents to like one another more. He could never just go to sleep and leave it to them to figure out what was happening and what to do about it. I said that at least as the baby and as himself in the dream, and maybe at times with me in our sessions, he can just leave it to me to know what is going on so he can sleep peacefully (knowing I am looking in on him to make sure everything is okay). Mr. S responded by saying that he had been able to jog today in a way that felt different. In the past the feeling in his legs would frighten him and he would stop after a very short time. "Today I felt all the fatigue in my legs. It wasn't that horrible feeling of being overwhelmed. Like the feeling I had on the couch at the end of last session, it was interesting."

Discussion

The fragments of the sessions just presented are not meant as models of analytic work with patients who have defensively created a disjunction between their minds and their bodies. Rather, I am attempting to talk to myself and to the reader about ways I found myself feeling and intervening that were surprising to me and that seemed to have been of value to this patient. To borrow the patient's words, I found myself feeling and behaving in ways that were curious and interesting to me.

Mr. S had spoken in an agitated way at the beginning of the session in which I made the two interventions that surprised me. He was furious at a "dimwit driver" who seemed to be paralyzed in a situation that he found overwhelming. The patient's disowned identification with the driver, and his displaced anger at me, were palpable in the room. Mr. S seemed to be frantically warding off his own feelings of confusion and helplessness. At first in that session I was unconsciously identifying with Mr. S in my efforts to defend myself against the full experience of being confused and flooded. I adopted the somewhat detached and contrived stance of the enlightened, knowledgeable psychoanalyst familiar with matters concerning child molestation.

It was necessary in that session, if any psychological work was to be done, for me to be able to "come to my senses," both in the sense of understanding what was going on, and perhaps even more important, in the sense of being able to live in, and speak from, my experience of my bodily sensations. This was an essential precondition for the patient's development of his own capacity to "come to his senses": to come to life in a physical/emotional/cognitive way. My own psychological work was done to a large extent in the medium of my reverie about helping my ten-month-old son to stand with his back to the wall of the closet so that his height could be recorded. The diabolical nature of the patient's "back to the wall" experience was made painfully and sadly real for me in an immediate sensory way as I unconsciously juxtaposed it with the loving "back to the wall" experience with my younger son. The measuring and the drawing of "permanent" markings on the wall were part of a family rite (with a living emotional/physical history) in which we all took pleasure. The tactile component of the reverie involved a sensory experience of the softness of my son's skin as I helped him stand up to be measured. It was from the sadness of this physically alive reverie that I said to Mr. S that when the molestation occurred he had been no taller than the table near the analytic couch.

It was only as I became increasingly able to be present in this sensory/emotional way that I could be more fully responsive to the patient's terror that he would never recover his sanity. It seems to me in retrospect that one of the most significant outcomes of having come more fully to my senses was my statement to the patient at the height of his fear of permanently going mad: "I won't let that happen." This was a spontaneous ("unminded") statement of a sort that I had never before made to Mr. S. It did not feel like a reassurance (which is a way of minimizing, and thus of refusing to join with the patient in an effort to face and to develop understandings of his psychic pain). Rather, it felt like a statement that I was making not only as a (transference-countertransference) parent, but as an analyst taking responsibility for the thinking and the clinical judgments that are part and parcel of analytic work with a patient struggling with psychotic-level anxiety and feelings of impending disintegration. My willingness to take on that responsibility seemed to facilitate the patient's capacity to experience the full intensity of his feelings. It was my responsibility to provide a reliable setting that ensured the patient's physical and psychological survival during this period of imminent fragmentation. I would not have made such a statement if I did not believe that as a consequence of my training and experience, I could provide the necessary physical and emotional presence during the hour, and in the days and months to follow. There is a very important practical aspect of providing an adequate analytic framework when working with patients on the edge of psychotic fragmentation. I had to know that I was both willing and able to be available to meet with the patient (both metaphorically and literally) as needed. (Meeting six or seven days a week for more than a year at a time have been necessary and extremely productive parts of my analytic work with other patients.)[1]

A second aspect of this session that seems to warrant examination was my asking the patient (again in an unplanned way) to imagine how his molestation experiences would feel at his present age. Although I have worked with many patients who experienced childhood sexual abuse, until the moment I made this intervention it had never occurred to me to imagine myself as an adult, and to ask the patient to imagine himself as an adult, into the eerily everyday quality of the molestation experience.

As I look back on the telling of this story and my invitation to the patient to be part of it, the experience seems to have served a number of physical/psychological functions. The sound of my voice speaking at some length was itself a form of (emotional/sensory) compassionate presence that was vital at that juncture. I was accompanying the patient psychologically (by inventing a story based on his experience) and physically (through the sound and feel of my voice) into the imagined scene. It was apparent to me, and I think to the patient, that I was

---

1. I do not believe that I could spontaneously have said to the patient, "I won't let that happen," had I not spent many years reading and rereading Winnicott's papers on the psyche-soma (1949) and the role of regression in the analytic process (1954). I am thinking in particular of the clinical vignette in which he says: "the patient became able to accept the not-knowing condition because I was [metaphorically] holding her and keeping a continuity by my own breathing while she let go, gave in, knew nothing" (1949, p. 252).

not only imagining the patient into the scene I was describing, but imagining myself into it as well, both in the
sense of identifying with him, and in the sense of introducing myself as a third figure bearing witness (and bearing
language, secondary-process thinking, and compassion).

The patient calmed in response to my invitation to
enter imaginatively into this story with me; his bodily
contortions gave way to a visibly relaxed muscular state.
Mr. S said that his head felt peaceful. He searched for a
word to describe his bodily sensations and at first settled
for the word "jazzed." I then introduced a somewhat
whimsical and quite flawed metaphor in which I likened
the transformation of feeling that Mr. S had just experienced to the downloading of computer data from his
head into his body. Mr. S laughed with obvious pleasure,
which in itself was an extremely rare event in the analysis. He went on to correct my weak metaphor: after trying
out a number of descriptive words that he felt incorrectly
described his bodily experience, he said that it was just
that he could feel that his body was there and that it was
a curious and interesting feeling, a feeling he liked.

Mr. S began the next session with his offhand comment about wanting to sleep on my couch, and then with
his dream, which ended: "I lay down on a bed next to the
crib and we slept." I was struck by the simplicity and tenderness of the words "we slept"—not "I went to sleep,"
or "I slept next to the baby," but "we slept." In putting it
in this way, Mr. S unselfconsciously captured a quality of
the analytic relationship at that point in the work: a feeling of one sleep (one "dream/reverie space") shared by

two separate people. The dream ended with the image
of a man coming into the room who looked like his childhood pediatrician but whom he knew, even in the dream,
to be me. The man looked on for a while, making sure
everything was okay, and then left. My interpretation of
the dream addressed the patient's feeling that in contrast
to the vigilant "mindedness" that had occupied so much
of his life from early childhood onward, he could (in
the dream, and sometimes in the sessions with me) "just
sleep," leaving it to me to make sure everything is okay.
Mr. S responded in a way that led me to feel that he was
ahead of me (as he had been earlier when he corrected
my "downloading" metaphor). He responded with an
account of being able to jog without fear of being overwhelmed by bodily sensation. This apparent non sequi-
tur seemed to me to be his unconscious way of saying to
both of us that not having to figure it out, "just sleeping,"
was an important experience for him in its own right,
and at the same time made possible something further:
a feeling-level "knowing" that he has a body—not a body
as idea or image, but a body alive with sensations such as
the feeling of fatigue in his legs as he jogs.

In sum, I have presented fragments of an analysis in
an effort to consider the origins and effects of two interventions that came as a surprise to me. The first of these
("I won't let that happen") involved speaking from a form
of "I-ness" (reflected in the voice with which I spoke) that
was new to me. It was a parental voice that took on the
responsibility of protectively "minding" the patient while
he was in a state of imminent psychotic fragmentation.

The second intervention involved my spontaneously inviting the patient to imagine himself into a story of molestation (based on his history and the history of the analysis) in which I was a third presence bearing witness, bearing language, and bearing compassion. Both interventions seemed to have had important consequences for the progress of the analysis. My spontaneous responses to the patient's psychotic-level anxiety and feelings of impending psychic disintegration seem to have contributed to a process in which he developed a greater sense of being alive in the experience of a coextensive minded body[2] and bodied mind.

2. I am grateful to Dr. Gloria Burk for the phrase "minded body." I find the term particularly apt not only for the way it locates the mind as an aspect of the body, but also for how it alludes to the infant's experience, when things are going well, of being "minded" (physically and emotionally cared for) by the mother over time.

7

An Elegy, a Love Song,
and a Lullaby

Prose states; poetry merely suggests. Poetry suggests because *what* it suggests cannot be stated. So it is to poetry that I turn, in this and several of the other chapters of this volume, in an effort to glean for myself and the reader a sense—and no more than a sense—of essences of important human experiences. The sense of an essence that we glean from a poem, if the poem is a good one, is not already there ("inside" the reader or "inside" the poem) waiting to be illuminated; it is newly created each time, not only in the medium of words, but just as important, in the medium of someone else's words. And that experience of being spoken by another person as one speaks him is a very large part of what is extraordinary and surprising and disturbing about poetry. We are known as we had not known ourselves because, up to that point, we had not been ourselves as fully as we are becoming in experiencing the poem and as the poem experiences us.

Similarly in the analytic relationship, patient and analyst as individuals each read and are read by the unconscious of the other. As a result, when the analysis is going well each participant is being known as he has not known himself—because he has not been as fully himself before.

In this volume, I have used the metaphor of conversations at the frontier of dreaming to convey—along with a great many other meanings—a sense of the way conscious and unconscious feelings give shape to language, and language gives shape to feelings. I will take up in this chapter one thread of those conversations, which concerns experiences of grieving as they are brought to life freshly, delicately, and unexpectedly in "Clearances" (1987), a poem Seamus Heaney wrote for his mother soon after her death. I will attempt to enter deeply into the poem and allow it to enter deeply into me—which is to enter into a variety of coexisting forms of love that shape an experience of grief.

A Life Divided

Before turning to "Clearances," which seems to me to be at once an elegy, a love song, and a lullaby, I will offer a brief narrative of Heaney's life as a context for reading his poem. For Heaney, as for most living writers in their artistic maturity, a biographical account is primarily the writer's account of his life as he would like it told. No biographer has yet provided a vantage point that signifi-

cantly enriches Heaney's own accounts of the important
events and currents of his life. Fortunately, this deficit is
to some extent offset by the three extraordinary collec-
tions of essays on poetry and his development as a poet
that Heaney (1980b, 1988a, 1995) has written over the
past twenty years.

Heaney describes himself as having lived from the
beginning of his life in a "space between." He was born
in 1939 at Mossbawn, a small, struggling family farm on
the edge of Londonderry, Northern Ireland.

> From the beginning, I was very conscious of bound-
> aries. There was a drain or stream, the Sluggan drain,
> an old division that ran very close to our house. It di-
> vided the townland of Tamniairn from the townland of
> Anahorish and those two townlands belonged in two
> different parishes . . . which are also in two different dio-
> ceses. . . . I was always going backwards and forwards.
> [Heaney attended a Catholic school in one parish and
> went to catechism in another.] I seemed always to be a
> little displaced; being in between was a kind of condi-
> tion, from the start. (Heaney, quoted by Corcoran 1986,
> p. 13)

"Being in between" may have been "a kind of condition" at home as well. The role of mother for Heaney and
his eight younger brothers and sisters was parceled out
among two women, Heaney's mother, Mary Kathleen,
and his aunt Mary. It is not surprising that Heaney, the

eldest, who saw eight siblings born into the family, felt always "a little displaced."[1]

It was not his mother but his Aunt Mary whom Heaney described in an interview as "the affectionate center [of the family]. I'm not saying in any way [Heaney protests] that my mother was distant, she was just always so busy with children; but Mary's function was almost entirely benign. She was the heart of the house in some ways" (Heaney, quoted in Corcoran 1986, p. 12).

The following written account captures something of the texture of Heaney's experience as a child living in-between:

> All children want to crouch in their secret nests. I loved
> the fork of a beech tree at the head of our lane, the close
> thicket of a boxwood hedge in the front of the house,
> the soft, collapsing pile of hay in a back corner of the
> byre; but especially I spent time in the throat of an old

---

1. I am aware of only two poems in Heaney's rather large opus that address in any depth his experiences with any of his siblings. One of these, the very early poem "Mid-Term Break" (1966a), concerns itself with Heaney's experience of the wake and viewing of a much younger brother, Christopher, who was accidentally hit and killed by a car. The poem is spoken in an oddly distant voice: "No gaudy scars, the bumper knocked him clear. / A four-foot box, a foot for every year" (p. 11). The other poem concerning one of Heaney's siblings is "Keeping Going" (1996), a somewhat guilt-laden tribute to his epileptic brother Hugh, who persevered into his adult life on the family farm: "My dear brother, you have good stamina. / You stay on where it happens" (p. 377).

willow tree at the end of the farmyard. It was a hollow tree, with gnarled, spreading roots, a soft, perishing bark and a pithy inside. Its mouth was like the fat and solid opening in a horse's collar, and, once you squeezed in through it, you were at the heart of a different life, looking out on the familiar yard as if it were suddenly behind a pane of strangeness. (Heaney 1978, pp. 17–18)

A great deal is happening in these few lines from "Mossbawn" (1978), a short piece that deserves the name *prose poem*. Between the large branches in the fork of the trunk of a beech tree, Heaney finds/creates a source, a secret nest; it is at once a thoroughly physical place and a place of the mind ("at the head"), a place of imagination. Virtually every word does double duty in this passage, as if poised between the physical and the imaginary; words are at the same time symbols and physical things themselves. "Crouch," for example, is both a verbal symbol and a pure sound, compacted as if squeezed into a small space; "thicket," "throat," and "pithy" are dense with bulky consonants packed tightly together around vowels that seem to be buried deep within; the "o" sounds in "opening," "horse's," and "collar" are themselves as we say them the physical sensation of our mouths opening to the hollow of our throats. In this passage, the sounds of a world and the sounds of words are coming at once from deep within the hollow of the throat of a tree, from the throat of the reader, and from the throats of Heaney's ancestors. These are "guttural" (Heaney 1979b, p. 155) sounds with gnarled, spreading roots that reach far into the ground and into history; yet they are part of the exciting, secret, scary immediacy of the personal, physical, imaginative presentness of Heaney's childhood.

Heaney's life as an adolescent became further disjointed and disconnected from itself when he was awarded a government grant to attend a private Catholic boarding school. Heaney recalls "just being bewildered" as a student at Queens University, Belfast, when the chairman of the English department suggested that he go on to pursue graduate work at Oxford. "My father and mother had absolutely no sense of [what] that [suggestion meant]. They wouldn't have stopped me, I'm not saying that [there is a lot Heaney says he is "not saying"], but the world I was moving in didn't have any direction for them, the compass needle just *wobbled*" (Heaney, quoted in Corcoran 1986, p. 19). As the eldest son of an Irish Catholic farming family of the North, Heaney would have been expected to become a farmer (like his father and his father's father), or perhaps a priest. His move from the rural life of farming to the life of a writer and poet was experienced by Heaney (and probably by his parents [Foster 1989]) as an act not only of independence, but also of self-imposed exile.

After graduating from Queens University, Heaney was awash in confusion and insecurity. He was in the grip of a conflict of loyalties: between his obligation and indebtedness to his family, and his feelings of membership in the Irish Catholic minority of Northern Ireland. "I suppose . . . that there was *some* expectation that I would earn [by working on the farm] . . . to pay something back to the home, you know" (Heaney, quoted by Corcoran 1986, p. 19). At the same time, Heaney's eyes and ears had been opened at University to the enormously rich literary heritage of the English language. It was a heritage he had no wish to disown. In fact, as a diffident University student, he had begun adding his own voice to it, publishing under a pseudonym some poems in the University literary magazine. Looking back on this period of his life ten years later, Heaney observed, "If you like, I began as a poet when my roots were crossed with my reading" (1972, p. 37).

Heaney's first collection of poems, *Death of a Naturalist* (1966b), received an extremely enthusiastic response from established English literary critics and from reviewers for the major Irish newspapers. During this period, Heaney was also active in the civil rights movement in Northern Ireland, where violence was steadily escalating.

A number of personal and political forces converged for Heaney in 1972 that would profoundly influence the succeeding decades of his life. On January 30 of that year, the day that came to be named "Bloody Sunday," the violence that Northern Ireland called "The Troubles" reached a new level of intensity when British paratroopers shot and killed thirteen unarmed Irish Catholic civil rights marchers in Londonderry. Three months later, Heaney resigned his post in the English department at Queens University, Belfast, and with his family, moved to a friend's cottage in a tiny rural village in County Wicklow in the

Republic of Ireland (about fifty miles south of Dublin). By this time, Heaney was a well-known poet and public figure, both in Northern Ireland and in the Republic. The Northern Irish newspaper *The Protestant Telegraph* delighted in the move of the "well-known papist propagandist [to] his spiritual home in the popish republic" (Corcoran 1986, p. 31). Heaney's arrival in the Republic was celebrated by an editorial in Dublin's *Irish Times* titled, "Ulster Poet Moves South" (p. 31).

Heaney's commentary, both written and in interviews, on the years immediately following the move to the Republic seem a bit removed from the pain that this decision must have caused him. In a 1979 interview, Heaney commented that he had felt that he would have been "compromising some part of myself" had he remained in the North after Bloody Sunday, as a consequence of "pressures [by the ruling Protestants] 'against' regarding the moment as critical." "To the Unionists it looked like a betrayal of the Northern thing" (Heaney, quoted in Corcoran 1986, p. 32). Heaney's reasoning and voice feel strained and defensive here.

The poetry that Heaney wrote just after the move to the Republic reflects profound ambivalence about the decision, including feelings of disloyalty and a sense of having passed up an irretrievable opportunity to be part of a critical moment of history. The poetry of this period is spoken in an intensely personal, though not confessional, voice. In "Exposure" (1975), the speaker asks himself, "How did I end up like this?" His response is a complex one that is itself an act of self-exposure:

> I am neither internee nor informer;
> An inner émigré, grown long-haired
> And thoughtful; a wood kerne
>
> Escaped from the massacre,
> Taking protective colouring
> From bole and bark, feeling
> Every wind that blows; (p. 136)

It would be a serious error to view Heaney as a poet of political protest, or even as a poet primarily driven by self-doubt concerning his role in the politics of Ireland. No one was more aware than Heaney that a poetry of political protest can easily become a disguised form of rhetorical prose. He found in his response to the "bog people"—the partially preserved centuries-old bodies interred in the Irish and Scandinavian peat bogs—a psychological place from which to write poems that address the humanness of both the murderer and the murdered. Many of the "bog people" had been killed in ceremonies of religious sacrifice.

The question of the relationship of poetry to the world in which it is written is a question to which Heaney returns again and again, as if always discontent with any articulation he makes. In his essay "The Government of the Tongue" (1986), he wrote that poetry disrupts the absolute givens, the received reality; it is

> a break with the usual life but not an absconding from it. Poetry . . . marks time in every possible sense of that

phrase. . . . It does not propose to be instrumental or effective. Instead, in the rift between what is going to happen and whatever we would wish to happen, poetry holds attention for a space, functions not as distraction but as pure concentration, a focus where our power to concentrate is concentrated back on ourselves. (p. 108)

In 1976, Heaney, his wife Marie, and their three children moved from County Wicklow to Dublin, where they have lived ever since. In the decades since then, Heaney has been honored by a series of awards for his poetry, and by appointments to professorships at Oxford and at Harvard. In 1995, he was awarded the Nobel Prize in literature.

In Memoriam M. K. H., 1911–1984

"Clearances," written in 1984, the year of the death of Heaney's mother, consists of a dedication, an epigraph poem, and eight sonnets. It has the quality of a collage— separate experiences of the poet with his mother, each one framing and speaking to the others. The movement of the poem is not the forward movement of time, but the backward and forward movement of the experience of coming to life in the act of mourning, which, to the degree the poem is successful, takes place in the acts of writing and reading the lines.

The Latin dedication, "*in memoriam* M. K. H., 1911– 1984," manages in a very compact way to sound a note of profound respect and sad irony that echoes through all

nine poems of "Clearances." Latin is the language of
Heaney the scholar, the professor, the poet, the man who
loves language and etymology, the person who can hear
the Latin and the French word *memor* (meaning "mindful" as well as "remembering") in the word *memoriam*. This
is a world incomprehensible to M. K. H. Latin is also the
world of M. K. H.'s Irish Catholicism, the language of the
Mass and of "the prayers for the dead" (sonnet III), of
religious belief and superstition (sonnet VI), of deep
social ties and violent division (sonnet I). For Heaney,
M. K. H.'s world of Latin was a world he could less and
less feel part of, but also a world he could never fully leave
(nor did he want to).

The epigraph poem revolves around a single delicately drawn metaphor in which the teaching of the secret
of splitting coal blocks is silently likened to the teaching
of the art of reading and writing poetry:

> *She taught me what her uncle once taught her:*
> *How easily the biggest coal block split*
> *If you got the grain and hammer angled right.*
>
> *The sound of that relaxed alluring blow,*
> *Its co-opted and obliterated echo,*
> *Taught me to hit, taught me to loosen,*
>
> *Taught me between the hammer and the block*
> *To face the music. Teach me now to listen,*
> *To strike it rich behind the linear black.*

A good deal of the poignancy of this poem lies in the
distance between what M. K. H. thought she was teach-

ing—or more likely did not think of as teaching at all—
and the enormity of the importance of her "lessons" to
Heaney the boy, the man, and the poet.

In the opening stanza, M. K. H. is the unselfconscious
conveyor of the accrued knowledge of generations. What
is being taught is a sensory and sensuous thing that can be
felt in the music of the language. The lines have a soft,
beautiful lilt to them, but there is also a quality of sturdi-
ness as the two opening lines each end with three consecutively stressed words: "once taught her" and "coal block
split." The words are alive with alliteration and repeated
word sounds: "biggest coal block," "get the grain," "taught
me/taught her," and so on. We can feel the sure-handed-
ness of the poet: a tautness of technique (Heaney's pun
on "taught" is no doubt intended) as Heaney gets the
rhythm and sound and meaning and syntax angled right.

And at the center of it all is the likening of the grain
of the coal block (derived from the layering in the earth
of innumerable millennia of once-living people, plants
and animals) and the grain of language (also derived
from the layering of millennia of living sounds and structures of spoken words and sentences). At the end of the
first stanza, the "secret" of the likening of the grain of the
coal and the grain of the language is playfully "given away"
as the words "grain and hammer" seem to whisper "grammar." The pleasure and delight and humor to be found
(made) in language are the pulse of this elegy. One of
the great achievements of "Clearances" is the way the pain
of grief is not in the least incompatible with taking pleasure in the language used to convey/create it. In fact, the

two experiences—the playfulness of the words and the sadness of the loss—are in this poem inseparable.

The movement from the first to the second stanza has the feel of moving through layerings of history and layerings of languages and layerings of feeling. The first stanza is chock- full of dense monosyllabic Anglo-Saxon words for everyday material things and actions—"taught," "hit," "got," "biggest," "coal," "block," "split," "grain," "hammer," "angled," "right." It is not until the second stanza that we hear the sound of another layer of the spoken language: the looser, more flowing Latin-derived words—"relaxed," "co-opted," and "obliterated"—that simultaneously refer to and have the sound and feel of process (as opposed to substantiality). The movement from the first to the second stanza is a movement from the touch and texture of M. K. H.'s hands and voice to a place a step removed. The first two lines of the second stanza are filled with words and meanings that both M. K. H. (I imagine) and I find difficult, opaque, confusing: What is a "relaxed alluring blow" or a "co-opted and obliterated echo"? The voice is a literary voice, a voice of the mind, not a "guttural" voice of the throat and the hands and the arms and the "got"/gut. I am tempted to try to pin down meanings in these lines. For instance, the word "co-opted" (meaning both to have elected to membership and to have stolen something from its intended place) might be read as reflecting Heaney's feeling that in writing his poetry (this poem), he co-opts (in both senses of the word) the language that his mother once taught him. In so doing he preserves her language by securing it membership in the body of English literature; yet in the very same act he uproots it, and in transporting it into his (now "removed") life of writing poems, "obliterates" even the echo of the sound of her words and sentences. Perhaps there is something to this reading, but to impose that set of meanings on these lines feels like my own act of obliterating their sound. I prefer to just let them be.

In the last two lines of the second stanza and in the third stanza, the speaker's voice takes on still another sound (not replacing the others, but adding to them). This is a voice that comes to life in a new way as (what I imagine to be) M. K. H.'s voice flickers in and out of Heaney's. The phrases "To face the music" and "To strike it rich" are aligned on the page at the beginning of lines 8 and 9, as if to emphasize their kinship. These phrases, which under other circumstances might feel like numbing clichés, are here made anew as the poem gives their original literal meanings a hearing. "To face the music" is an expression coined in the musical theater; it refers to the courage it takes for an actor to look out over the orchestra pit to face the audience and sing his song. (It requires considerable daring for a son to write a poem that attempts to do justice to the full complexity of who his mother was and is to him and what it feels like to miss her.) And "To strike it rich" has a childlike gusto and innocence to it, a way of referring to the best thing that could possibly happen; at the same time, the phrase has the muscular strength of a pick ploughing into stone, seeking a vein of ore. And we feel in our mouths the pick against the stone as the tongue strikes the palate again and again as we say the words "taught" (repeated three times in two lines), "to" (repeated four times), "hit," "between," "teach," and "strike." It is as if the feel of the words in our mouths has something of the feel of the coarse fiber and steady rhythm of the day-to-day life of a mother of nine, living and working on a small impoverished farm in County Derry.

That phrase in particular—"to strike it rich"—whether it is Heaney's or his mother's or both, is set off in bold relief by the poem's final words, which follow it directly: "behind the linear black." These words are unmistakably Heaney's. M. K. H. would never have used these "poetic," literary words. ("You know all them things," M. K. H. is heard saying in sonnet IV.) The words "behind the linear black" quietly suggest not only the grain of the coal block, and the grain of language, but also the black of the ink making up the lines of the poem on the page, and the linear black of the line formed by the train of mourners dressed in black following behind the casket in M. K. H.'s funeral procession.

The divide between Heaney's life as a poet and his mother's life is almost bridged in this poem as he tries to get the sound of his feelings angled right against the grain of the language. But his attempt to bridge the gap is not a serious one—the gap cannot be bridged, nor should it be. That space between Heaney and M. K. H. is a clearance, "utterly empty, utterly a source" (sonnet VIII) in which Heaney lives and grieves and writes his poems.

As If Nothing Had Happened

I will now look closely at the fifth of the eight sonnets of
"Clearances"—the one I am most fond of, a poem that
encompasses an extraordinary range and depth of feeling:

The cool that came off sheets just off the line
Made me think the damp must still be in them
But when I took my corners of the linen
And pulled against her, first straight down the hem
And then diagonally, then flapped and shook
The fabric like a sail in a cross-wind,
They made a dried-out undulating thwack.
So we'd stretch and fold and end up hand to hand
For a split second as if nothing had happened
For nothing had that had not always happened
Beforehand, day by day, just touch and go,
Coming close again by holding back
In moves where I was X and she was O
Inscribed in sheets she'd sewn from ripped-out flour sacks.

This sonnet, like all of Heaney's successful poems,
is written in the "Irish language," not in Gaelic, of
course, but in a form of English that is saturated with
the sounds and rhythms of Gaelic as well as the wealth
of metaphors that are descendants of Gaelic mythology,
literature, and everyday speech.[2] Consequently, saying

---

2. All Irish children were taught Gaelic in school when Heaney was
a child. Even at present Gaelic is taught throughout every child's

Heaney's poems aloud poses many of the same problems that come up in saying aloud poems written in any foreign tongue with which the reader has some familiarity, but is far from fluent. This is readily apparent when one hears Heaney read his own poems—for instance, in the recording *Stepping Stones* (1988b). The words and the meanings of the words in sonnet V, for example, are linked by their sounds when said by Heaney in ways that are far more interesting than when I say them. When spoken by Heaney, the word "cool" in line 1 rhymes with (pulls on) "pulled" in line 4 (which he pronounces almost as "pooled"), which chimes with "moves" (line 13) and "sewn" (line 14). "Sewn" is pronounced as a two-syllable word with a vowel sound leaning toward that of "soon," which carries into the vowel sound of "un" ("oon") in "undulating" (line 7), and is linked with "always" in line 10 (pronounced "ulways"), which in turn is picked up in the next line by the wonderful series of vowel sounds "just touch and go" (pronounced "just tutch ind goo").

The rhythm of the "Irish language" (as spoken and written by Heaney) is distinctive. In English, the opening line of the sonnet, for instance, might be said with a more or less iambic (da *dum*, da *dum*, da *dum*) beat that approximates the rhythm of walking. But in Gaelic as well as in present-day Irish, stressed syllables seem (to the English-speaking ear) to pop up unexpectedly (for example, by

---

school-years, though in fact few learn to read or speak it with more than minimal proficiency.

accenting the word "off" both times it occurs in the first line). As a result, Irish seems to skip irregularly, like a stone skimming over the surface of a pond, while English more often seems to prefer to amble (and, at its worst, to trudge).

Sonnet V is the most sensuous of the poems in "Clearances." It creates a world where sensations are the stuff of experience. For instance, in the first two lines, the adjectives "cool" and "damp," which ordinarily describe other things, are here the things themselves ("the cool" and "the damp"). I have no doubt that Heaney was aware that "cool" might refer not only to sheets but also to the body of the dead, and that "damp" might suggest female sexual excitement. And yet the feel of the poem is such that only a "predator," as Ricks (1979, p. 98) has put it, would seize upon these meanings, and in so doing needlessly make heavy-handed a poem that is nothing if not delicate.

The action of the language of the poem is "all go." The movement is the continuous rhythmic movement of two people folding sheets—each line moves into the next, slowing only slightly at the end of each line. The poet, clearly in command of the language, is as sure-handed at his work as his mother was at hers. The "corners" of the poem (the line-ending words) are gathered end to end by the soft, alternating end rhymes of "line" and "linen," "them" and "hem," "shook" and "thwack," "wind" and "hand," and so on. There is at the same time a visual folding of words (words that are not only symbols but things) as "them" is folded into "hem," "linen" into "line."

The word "think" (in the phrase "Made me think the damp must still be in them") quietly underscores the fact that what is happening in the poem is the opposite of thinking: it is an experience of wordless feeling—all sensation, all part of the inarticulate present moment, and yet paradoxically created entirely in the medium of words. The words, as if of their own accord "unthinkingly," seem to create unselfconscious, imaginative metaphors. Metaphor in this poem seems to come off the line as invisibly as the cool comes off the bedsheets just off the clothesline. (How clunky and plodding the poem becomes in paraphrase when the lines are weighed down with an extra load of words such as "bed" and "clothes.")

A good part of what is most alive for me about the first seven-line sentence is the way the ease and decorum of the ceremony of folding sheets (reflected in the well-behaved rhyme scheme and iambic meter of the stately sonnet form) is disturbed by the single unassuming word "her" in the phrase "pulled against her." The word "her" is used in place of the expected word "hers" ("my corners" pulled against hers). The word "her" (her felt body and her felt being) is unexpectedly sensuous (and yet sacred), like a first kiss in which there is as much holding back as letting go. The sensuousness is further enhanced as "her" is folded into the quietly erotic word "hem," which looks Janus-faced to both the fully known mother folding sheets and the unfathomable, bodied femininity of a mother wearing skirts.

The second half of the poem is spoken in a different voice:

So we'd stretch and fold and end up hand to hand
For a split second as if nothing had happened
For nothing had that had not always happened

Beforehand, day by day, just touch and go,
Coming close again by holding back
In moves where I was X and she was O
Inscribed in sheets she'd sewn from ripped-out flour sacks.

The shift in the voice here is in part a reflection of
the change in the pace of the poem in its second half. The
clauses of the first sentence seem to fly like sheets "in a
cross-wind," pinned to the line by conjunctions that create a sense of rapid forward movement: "But when I took,"
"and pulled," "first," "and then," "then flapped and shook."

The "So" that begins the second sentence of the
poem is not so much a conjunction of sequence as it is a
pause in the flow of the poem. Although "So" has a single
syllable, it is a soft syllable of long duration, especially in
contrast to the crispness of the word "thwack" that immediately precedes it. The slowing of the pace of the
poem opens a calm space between the words. The rhythmic to-and-fro of "we'd stretch and fold and end up"
naturally flows into (ends up with) the very ordinary,
seemingly inevitable words "hand to hand"—which change
everything! The electricity of the moment crackles and
sends the poem reeling, giving and taking back as it goes:

For a split second as if nothing had happened
For nothing had that had not always happened
Beforehand . . .

No paraphrase can do justice to these lines. The
words and phrases of a good poem (as Frost [1936] liked
to say) "talk to each other" (p. 427), but here the voices

all seem to be talking at once in the excitement and shyness of the swirling, confused and confusing feelings of the experience not simply of love but of being in love. We feel and hear in the voice of the speaker both the voice of the boy's protestations and the voice of the man compassionately remembering the tenderness and wildness of that moment in which "nothing had happened / For nothing had that had not always happened."

And at the same time, something else, something much quieter, can be heard behind all the commotion of secretly, transparently, being in love. Tacked onto the flurry of nothings and always is the word "Beforehand," which, like "So" three lines earlier, slows the poem down, creating a clearance in which the sound of the word "Beforehand" lingers. The clearance generated by the word "Beforehand" is an experience that precedes writing ("before hand"). It is an experience that had "always happened" before hands when we were all skin and arms and legs and cheeks and bottoms and breasts and backs—before we had hands that could end up hand to hand with her hands. That time, beforehand, was a time before words, when we lived in inarticulate feeling, in the conversation of sounds made by a baby and his mother. The beauty of the music of those sounds is nowhere more audible than in the gently swaying sound of the poem singing as if to itself, a song that is both lullaby and love song:

Beforehand, day by day, just touch and go,
Coming close again by holding back
In moves where I was X and she was O
Inscribed in sheets she'd sewn from ripped-out flour sacks.

There is a wonderful sensory pleasure in saying the consecutive phrases "day by day, just touch and go" as the tongue hits the palate for a split second—just touch and go. In this bodily experience, the difference between the pleasure of a baby sucking and cooing and the pleasure and excitement of a boy's first being in love and first kiss flow into and out of one another. And again, in the line that follows: "Coming close again while holding back," speaks at the same time to the boy's amorous dance with his mother and to the baby's and the mother's "Coming close again" as she is "holding [his] back."

In the final two lines of the poem, the metaphor of the game of tic-tac-toe is inscribed in the metaphor of folding sheets. The game, like the poem, is a highly structured form of playing with letters and words. Within the game, the words seem to take on a life of their own and speak for themselves—for example, as "I was X and she was O" whispers the forbidden word *sex* in the elision of "was" and "X." (I am reminded of my four-year-old son's coming home from nursery school and whispering, blushing, that the girls were wearing "leotards"—knowing that I would understand the true meaning of the word and the need for shared secrecy.)

The final line of the poem—"Inscribed in sheets she'd sewn from ripped-out flour sacks"—is remarkable for the power and complexity of feeling it conveys/creates. There is playfulness and music in the first half of the line in the sequence of "s" and "n" sounds in groupings of words of parallel structure: "Inscribed in sheets she'd sewn." But the heavy iambic beat of the line—da *dum*, da *dum*, da *dum*, reminiscent of a child's song—changes in the second half of the line into a cadence closer to the sound of the ordinary spoken words of an adult: "from ripped-out flour sacks." It is as if the vantage point of the boy being (or more accurately, coming into being) with his mother is transformed into the vantage point of the man seeing his mother and himself from an enormous distance of time and space.

While the predominant movement of the poem up until its final line has been from the real to the meta-phorical—from the clothesline to the poetic line—the tide shifts in the final line, and now is moving forcefully from the metaphorical to the real. The "sheets" on the line were transformed by the poet in line 1 into pages of a book of poems. The sheets in the final line of the poem seem no longer to be willing to lend themselves to clever wordplay. The sheets are now sheets, simply bedsheets, that "she'd sewn from ripped-out flour sacks." The word "ripped-out" creates, in the density and edgedness of its consonants and in its compression of two words into one, the force (even the violence) of the speaker's feelings of grief, which in this line involve an experience of having something (someone) torn out of him.

It is as if Heaney's experience of the full realness of M. K. H. has been postponed—or perhaps has not been possible—until the final line of the poem. In the poem's final phrase there is an enormous depth of sadness and love and admiration as "M. K. H., 1911–1984" is experienced as a person "not found in verse" (Borges 1960b, p. 131): Heaney's mother, the mother of nine children (one dead), attempting to make do with bedsheets "she'd sewn from ripped-out flour sacks."

And yet, this elegy/love song/lullaby refuses to come to rest in any single strand of feeling. Heaney manages to achieve in the ending of this sonnet the verbal equivalent of a musical chord. "Flour," the food-stuff, is at the same time, in the same sound, the much lighter and more evanescent "flower." Mourning too is multifaceted: it is the stuff of the "prayers for the dying," the ceremony of the Requiem Mass, the linear black of the funeral procession, the centuries-old sonnet-form. At the same time, mourning, like a flower, is a "useless," very living, very loving thing, which in this line is a gift that a boy/man shyly (while no one is watching) gives his mother at the very last moment. The experience of M. K. H.'s death, as created in the movement of the language of this poem and in "Clearances" as a whole, is the most extraordinary and the most ordinary of human events, "for nothing had that had not always happened / Beforehand. . . ."

I will end not with the last of the series of poems comprising "Clearances," but with an "earlier" moment (in sonnet VII), an eternally recurring moment that is no earlier and no later than any other moment in the continuous movement of being born and being left, of being filled and being felled, of keeping close and being kept.

. . . Then she was dead,
The searching for a pulsebeat was abandoned
And we all knew one thing by being there.
The space we stood around had been emptied
Into us to keep, it penetrated
Clearances that suddenly stood open.
High cries were felled and a pure change happened.

8

Reading Winnicott

Psychoanalysis in its first century has had several great thinkers, but, to my mind, only one great English-speaking writer: D. W. Winnicott. Because style and content are so interdependent in his writing, his papers are not well served by thematic reading aimed exclusively at gleaning what the paper is "about." Such efforts often result in trivial aphorisms. Winnicott, for the most part, does not use language to arrive at conclusions; rather, he uses language to create experiences in reading that are inseparable from the ideas he is presenting—or, more accurately, the ideas he is playing with.

I offer here a reading of Winnicott's (1945) "Primitive Emotional Development": a paper containing the seeds of virtually every major contribution to psychoanalysis that he would make over the course of the succeeding twenty-six years of his life. I hope to demonstrate the interdependence of the life of the ideas being devel-

oped and the life of the writing in this seminal contribution to the analytic literature. What Winnicott's paper
has to offer to an analytic reader could not be said in any
other way (which is to say that the writing is extraordi-
narily resistant to paraphrase). It is my experience that
an awareness of the way the language is working significantly enhances what one can learn from reading
Winnicott.

In recent years, I have found that the only way I can
do justice to studying and teaching Winnicott is to read
his papers aloud, line by line, as I would a poem, exploring what the language is doing in addition to what it is
saying. It is not an overstatement to say that a great many
passages from Winnicott's papers could well be called
prose poems. These passages meet Tom Stoppard's
(1999) definition of poetry as "the simultaneous compression of language and expansion of meaning" (p. 10).

In my discussion of Winnicott's paper, I will not limit
myself to an explication of the text, although many of the
ideas developed there will be discussed. My principal
interest is in looking at this paper as a piece of nonfiction
literature, in which the meeting of reader and writing
generates an imaginative experience in the medium of
language. To speak of Winnicott's writing as literature is
not to minimize its value as a way of conveying ideas that
have proved to be of enormous importance to the
development of psychoanalytic theory and practice. On
the contrary, my effort is to demonstrate how the life of
the writing is critical to, and inseparable from, the life
of the ideas.

Before looking closely at "Primitive Emotional Development," I will offer a few observations about Winnicott's writing that are relevant to the whole of his opus. The first of these to strike the reader is its form; Winnicott's papers, unlike those of any other psychoanalyst I can think of, are brief (usually six to ten pages in length). They often contain a moment in the middle of the paper when he takes the reader aside and tells him, in a single sentence, "the essential feature of my communication is this…" (Winnicott 1971a, p. 50). But the most distinctive signature of Winnicott's writing is the voice. It is casual and conversational, but always profoundly respectful of both the reader and the subject matter. The speaking voice gives itself permission to wander, yet has the compactness of poetry; it has an extraordinary intelligence, yet one that is genuinely humble and well aware of its limitations; there is a disarming intimacy that at times takes cover in wit and charm; the voice is playful and imaginative, but never folksy or sentimental.

Any effort to convey a sense of the voice in Winnicott's writing must locate at its core the quality of playfulness, and there is an enormous range of forms of playfulness to be found. To name only a few, there are the unselfconscious feats of imaginative and compassionate understanding in his accounts of "squiggle games" (1971c) with his child patients. There is the serious playfulness (or playful seriousness) of Winnicott's efforts to generate a form of thinking/theorizing that is adequate to the paradoxical nature of human experience as he understands it. Winnicott takes delight in subtle word play—for instance, in this repetition of a familiar phrase in slightly different forms in referring to a patient's need to begin and to end analysis: "I do analysis because that is what the patient needs to have done and to have done with" (1962, p. 166).

While his writing is personal, the voice has a certain English reserve that befits the paradoxical combination of formality and intimacy that is a hallmark of psychoanalysis (Ogden 1989b). In all of these matters of form and voice, Winnicott's work holds strong resemblances to the compact, intelligent, playful, at times charming, at times ironic, always irreducible writing of Borges's *Ficciones* (1944) and Frost's prose and poetry.

Winnicott's inimitable voice can be heard almost immediately in "Primitive Emotional Development" as he explains his "methodology":

> I shall not first give an historical survey and show the development of my ideas from the theories of others; because my mind does not work that way. What happens is that I gather this and that, here and there, settle down to clinical experience, form my own theories and then, last of all, interest myself in looking to see where I stole what. Perhaps this is as good a method as any. (p. 145)

There is playful wit to the words, "Perhaps this is as good a method as any." This seemingly tacked-on afterthought expresses the central theme of the paper as a whole—creating "a method," a way of being alive that suits the individual and becomes his unique "watermarking"

(Heaney 1980a, p. 47), is perhaps the single most important outcome of primitive emotional development. In the
process of coming into being as an individual, the infant
(with the "invisible" assistance of the mother) "gather[s]
this and that, here and there." Early experience of self is
fragmented, and at the same time is (with the mother's
help) "gather[ed]" in a way that allows the infant's experience of self, now and again, to come together in one
place. Moreover, for the infant, the bits of others (intro-
jects)—or for the writer, the ideas of other writers—must
not be allowed to take over the process of creating meaning. "My mind does not work that way," nor does that of
a healthy infant in the care of a healthy mother. The
individual's own lived experience must be the basis
for creating coherence *for* one's self and integrity *of* oneself. Only after a sense of self has begun to come into
being (for the infant and for the writer), can one acknowledge the contributions of others to the creating of oneself (and one's ideas): "last of all [I] interest myself in
looking to see where I stole what."

Winnicott then briefly discusses several aspects of the
analytic relationship, with particular emphasis on the
transference-countertransference. He believes that this
body of experience is a major source of his conception of
primitive emotional development. I will examine only one
brief passage—two sentences, to be precise—of Winnicott's
discussion of the transference-countertransference. I have
selected these sentences because I find them to be of great
importance both to the understanding of Winnicott's conception of the workings of the analytic relationship, and

with regard to the powerful interdependence of language
and ideas in Winnicott's work:

> The depressed patient requires of his analyst the under-
> standing that the analyst's work is to some extent his
> effort to cope with his own (the analyst's) depression, or
> shall I say guilt and grief resultant from the destructive
> elements in his own (the analyst's) love. To progress
> further along these lines, the patient who is asking for
> help in regard to his primitive, pre-depressive relation-
> ship to objects needs his analyst to be able to see the
> analyst's undisplaced and co-incident love and hate of
> him. (pp. 146–147)

In the opening clause of the first of these two sentences, Winnicott offers not only a theory of depression
radically different from that of Freud or Klein, but also a
new conception of the role of countertransference in the
psychoanalytic process. He is suggesting here that depression is not, most fundamentally, a pathological identification with the hated aspect of an ambivalently loved (and
lost) object, unconsciously designed to preserve and protect the loved aspect of the object and to deny its loss
(Freud 1914b). Neither does the understanding of depression that Winnicott is suggesting view depression as
centered around the unconscious fantasy that one's anger
has injured, driven away, or killed the loved object (Klein
1952).

In the space of a single sentence, Winnicott suggests
(by his *use of the idea* rather than by his explication of it)

that depression is a manifestation of the patient's taking on as his own—in fantasy, taking into himself—his mother's depression (or that of other loved objects) with the unconscious aim of relieving her of her depression. What is astounding is that this conception of the patient's depression is presented not in a direct statement, but by means of a sentence that is virtually incomprehensible unless the reader does the work of creating/discovering for himself the conception of the intergenerational origins and dynamic structure of depression. Only after the reader has done this work does it begin to make sense why "The depressed patient requires of his analyst the understanding that the analyst's work is to some extent his effort to cope with his own (the analyst's) depression" (Winnicott 1945, pp. 146–147).[1] In other words, if the analyst is unable to cope with the feelings of depression (both normative and pathological) that arise from his own past and current life experiences, he will not be able to recognize (to feel in the moment) the ways in which the patient unconsciously is attempting to, and to some degree is succeeding in, taking on the depression of the analyst-as-transference-mother.

---

1. The term "depression," as it is used in this sentence, seems to refer to a wide spectrum of psychological states ranging from clinical depression to the universal depression associated with the achievement of the depressive position (Klein 1952). The latter is a normative stage of development and "mode of generating experience" (Ogden 1989b, p. 9) involving whole object relatedness, ambivalence, and a deep sense of loss in recognizing one's separateness from one's mother.

The aspects of the analyst's depression that arise from sources independent of his unconscious identification with the patient's depressed internal object mother are far less available to the patient's ministerings, because the patient cannot find in the analyst the depression of his (the patient s) mother which for nearly the whole of his life he has intimately known and attended to. The patient is single-mindedly concerned with the depression that is unique to his own internal object mother. (Each person's depression is his or her own unique creation, rooted in the particular circumstances of his or her own life experience and personality organization.) Winnicott is suggesting that the analyst must cope with his own depression in order that he may experience the patient's (internal object) mother's depression (which is being projected into him). Only if he is able to contain/live with the experience of the (internal object) mother's depression (as distinct from his own) will he be able to experience the patient's pathological effort to relieve the mother's psychological pain (now felt to be located in the analyst) by introjecting it into himself (the patient) as a noxious foreign body.

The second clause of this sentence, while introduced by Winnicott as if it were simply another way of saying what he has already said in the first clause ("or shall I say"), is in fact something altogether new: "[The analyst of a depressed patient must cope with his own] guilt and grief resultant from the destructive elements in his own (the analyst's) love" (p. 147). Thus, the analyst of the depressed patient must also be able to live with the inevitable destructiveness of love, in the sense that love makes a demand on the loved person that may (in fantasy and, at times, in reality) be too much of a strain for that person. In other words, the analyst, in the course of his personal analysis and by means of his ongoing self-analysis, must come to terms with his own fears of the draining effects of his love sufficiently to be able to love his patient without fear that such feelings will harm the patient and thereby cause himself (the analyst) "guilt and grief." (I am aware of the awkwardness of my own language in discussing this passage. These ideas are difficult to convey partly because of the extreme compactness of Winnicott's language and partly because Winnicott has not yet fully worked out the ideas he is presenting. Moreover, the ideas he is developing involve irresolvable emotional contradictions and paradoxes: the analyst must be sufficiently free of depression to experience the depression which the depressed patient projects into him. The analyst must also be able to love without fear of the toll that his love takes—for if the analyst is frightened of the destructive effects of his own love, there is little chance of his analyzing the patient's fears of the taxing/destructive effects of his love on the analyst.

Winnicott does not stop here. In the sentence that follows, he revolutionizes (and I use the word advisedly) the conception of the "analytic frame" by viewing it as a medium for the expression of the analyst's hatred of the patient: "the end of the hour, the end of the analysis, the rules and regulations, these all come in as important expressions of [the analyst's] hate" (p. 147). The analytic reader recognizes immediately as truth and as part of his experience with almost every patient that these actions (so ordinary that they frequently go unnoticed) are expressions of the analyst's hate. Winnicott is recognizing/interpreting the unspoken expressions of hate that the analyst/reader unconsciously and preconsciously experiences (often accompanied by feelings of relief) in "throwing the patient out" (by punctually ending each meeting) and in establishing the limits of what he will provide the patient (by maintaining the other aspects of the analytic frame). Implicit here is the notion that the analyst's fear of the destructiveness of his hatred of the patient may lead to treatment-destructive breaches of the analytic frame: for example, extending the session for more than a few minutes in order "not to cut the patient off," or setting the fee at a level below what the patient can afford "because the patient has been consistently exploited by his parents in childhood," or reflexively telephoning the patient when the patient has missed a session "to be sure he is all right," and so on.

Only by looking closely at these sentences can one discern and appreciate what is going on in the living relationship between writing and reader that constitutes so much of the life of the ideas being developed. As we have seen, the writing demands that the reader become an active partner in the creation of meaning. The writing (like the communications of an analysand) suggests, and only suggests, possibilities of meaning (Kohon 1999). The reader/analyst must be willing and able not to know, and in so doing make room in himself for the experience/

creation of a number of possible meanings to be experienced/created, and to allow one meaning or another, or several meanings concurrently, to achieve ascendance (for a time).

Moreover, it is important to note that the writing "works" (to borrow a word from Winnicott's statement of his "method") in large measure through its power to understand (to correctly interpret the unconscious of) the reader. Perhaps all good writing (whether in poems, plays, novels, or essays) to a significant degree "works" in this way.

Winnicott's writing in the paper under discussion (and in almost all of the papers included in his three major volumes of collected papers (1958, 1965, 1971d) is surprisingly short on clinical material. This, I believe, is a consequence of the fact that the "clinical experience" is to such a large degree located in the reader's experience of "being read" (that is, of being interpreted, understood) by the writing. When Winnicott does offer clinical material, he often refers not to a specific intervention with a particular patient, but to a "very common experience" (1945, p. 150) in analysis. In this way, he implicitly asks the reader to draw on his own lived experience with patients: not for the purpose of "taking in" Winnicott's ideas, but to invite from the reader "original response" (Frost 1942a, p. 307).

Still other forms of generative interplay of style and content, of writing and reader, take on central importance in a passage a bit later in the paper that addresses

experiences of unintegration and integration in early
development:

> An example of unintegration phenomena is provided by
> the very common experience of the patient who proceeds
> to give every detail of the week-end and feels contented
> at the end if everything has been said, though the analyst
> feels that no analytic work has been done. Sometimes we
> must interpret this as the patient's need to be known in
> all his bits and pieces by one person, the analyst. To be
> known means to feel integrated at least in the person of
> the analyst. This is the ordinary stuff of infant life, and an
> infant who has had no one person to gather his bits to-
> gether starts with a handicap in his own self-integrating
> task, and perhaps he cannot succeed, or at any rate can-
> not maintain integration with confidence. . . .
> There are long stretches of time in a normal infant's
> life in which a baby does not mind whether he is many
> bits or one whole being, or whether he lives in his mother's
> face or in his own body, provided that from time to time
> he comes together and feels something. (1945, p. 150)

Implicit in this passage is the recognition of the
analyst's anger at patients who "give every detail of the
week-end," leaving the analyst with the feeling "that no
analytic work has been done." Winnicott leaves it entirely
to the reader to imagine the analyst's impulse to dump
his anger and feelings of failure back into the patient in
the form of a resistance interpretation ("You seem to be

filling the hour with details that serve to defeat any possibility of analytic work getting done" [my example]).

Winnicott then provides the reader with a major revision of analytic technique. He accomplishes this so subtly that the reader is apt not to notice it if he is not attending carefully to what is going on in the writing. Nothing short of a new way of being with and talking to patients is being offered, without preaching or fanfare, to the reader: "Sometimes we must interpret[2] this [the patient's giving every detail of his week-end] as the patient's need to be known in all his bits and pieces by one person, the analyst." The phrase, "Sometimes we must," addresses the reader as a colleague who is familiar with the clinical situation being described, and who very likely has felt it necessary to intervene in the way Winnicott is describing. Perhaps the reader/analyst has not fully named for himself what he has been experiencing and doing with his patient. The language does not debunk the angry resistance interpretation that the reader/analyst has either made or has been inclined to make in response to his feelings of frustration and failure. Winnicott, by means of the language he uses to address the reader, provides *an experience in reading* that helps the reader undefensively to gather together his own unarticulated experiences from his own analysis and from his analytic work with his patients.

---

2. It seems that Winnicott is referring here to silent interpretations that the analyst formulates in words for himself in the moment, and may at a later time present to the patient.

Moreover, the simple phrase "very common experience" conveys an important theoretical concept (again without calling attention to itself): primitive states of unintegration are not restricted to the analysis of severely disturbed patients; such states regularly occur in the analysis of all of our patients, including the healthiest ones. This writing "technique" does not have the feel of a manipulation; rather, it feels like a good interpretation. It is a statement that puts into words what the reader/analyst has known from his experience all along—but has not known that he has known it, and has not known it in the verbally symbolized, integrated way that he currently is coming to know it.

The second paragraph of the passage being discussed is remarkable:

> There are long stretches of time in a normal infant's life in which a baby does not mind whether he is many bits or one whole being, or whether he lives in his mother's face or in his own body, provided that from time to time he comes together and feels something.

This sentence is distinctive, not only for the originality of the ideas it develops, but also for the way its syntax participates in a sensory way to the creation of those ideas. The sentence is constructed of many (I count ten) groups of words that are read with a very brief pause between them (for instance, a pause after the words "time," "life," "mind," and so on). The sentence not only states, but brings to life in its own audible structure, the experience of living in bits ("for a long time") in a meandering sort of way before coming together (for a moment) in its final two bits: "he comes together" and "feels something." The voice, syntax, and rhythm, and the carefully chosen words and expressions that constitute this sentence—working together as they do with the ideas being developed—create an experience in reading that is as distinctively Winnicott as the opening paragraph of *The Sound and the Fury* is distinctively Faulkner, or as the opening sentence of *The Portrait of a Lady* is uniquely Henry James.

The reader of the sentence being discussed is not moved to question how Winnicott can possibly know what an infant feels, or to point out that regressions in the analyses of children and adults (whether psychotic, depressed, or quite healthy) bear a very uncertain correlation with infantile experience. Rather, the reader is inclined to suspend disbelief for a time and to enter into the experience of reading (with Winnicott) and to allow himself to be carried by the music of the language and ideas. The reader lives an experience in the act of reading that is something like that of the imagined infant, who does not mind whether he is many bits (experiencing a floating feeling that accompanies nonlinear thinking) or one whole being (experiencing a "momentary stay against confusion" [Frost 1939, p. 777]). Winnicott's writing, like a guide "who only has at heart your getting lost" (Frost 1947, p. 341), ensures that we will never get it right in any final way, and we do not mind.

Subliminally, the pun on "mind" allows the clause, "a baby does not mind whether he is many bits or one whole being," to concentrate into itself different overlapping meanings. The baby "does not mind" because the mother is there "minding" him (taking care of him). And he "does not mind" in that he feels no pressure to be "minded"— that is, to create premature, defensive mindedness which is disconnected from bodily experience. In punning, the writing itself deftly and unselfconsciously creates just such an experience of the pleasure of not minding, of not having to know, of not having to pin down meaning—and thus being able simply to enjoy the liveliness of a fine experience in the medium of language and ideas.

The language that Winnicott uses to describe the infant's coming together in one place is surprising in that the "place" where coming together occurs is not a place at all, but an action (the act of feeling something). Moreover, the infant, in "coming together," does not simply feel—he "feels something" (Winnicott 1945, p. 150). The word "something" has a delightful ambiguity to it. "Something" is a concrete thing, the object that is felt; at the same time, "something" is the most indefinite of words suggesting only that some feeling is experienced. This delicate ambiguity creates in the experience of reading the flickering of the feeling-world of the infant: a world loosely bound to objects, loosely localized, experienced now in the body as objectless sensation, now in the more defined and localized sensation of feeling an object, now in the mother's face.[3]

---

3. The role played by the word "something" in this sentence is reminiscent of Frost's use of nouns to invoke simultaneously the myste-

The unexpected turns, the quiet revolutions in this early Winnicott paper are too numerous to address. I cannot resist, however, taking a moment simply to marvel at the way in which Winnicott, the pediatrician, the child-analyst, nonchalantly jettisons the accrued technical language of fifty years of psychoanalytic writing in favor of language that is alive with the experiences he is describing:

> . . . there are the quiet and the excited states. I think an infant cannot be said to be aware at the start that while feeling this and that in his cot or enjoying the skin stimulations of bathing, he is the same as himself screaming for immediate satisfaction, possessed by an urge to get at and destroy something unless satisfied by milk. This means that he does not know at first that the mother he is building up through his quiet experiences is the same as the power behind the breasts that he has in his mind to destroy. (p. 151)

The infant has his quiet and his excited states—everyone who has spent time with a baby knows this, but why had no one thought to put it this way? The baby feels "this and that" (there is ease in the language as there is

---

rious and the utterly concrete and mundane: for example, in lines such as "Something there is that doesn't love a wall" (1914b, p. 39); or "One had to be versed in country things / Not to believe the phoebes wept" (1923a, p. 223); or "What was that whiteness? / Truth? A pebble of quartz? For once, then, something" (1923b, p. 208).

ease in the baby's state of mind-body) and enjoys the "skin stimulations of bathing" and "cannot be said to be aware [in the quiet states] . . . that . . . he is the same as himself screaming for immediate satisfaction." (And how better to convey the feeling of continuity of identity across discontinuous feeling/meaning states than with unobtrusive alliteration of "s" sounds—sixteen times in one sentence —in words carrying a very wide range of meaning, including: "states," "start," "skin," "stimulation," "same," "screaming," "satisfaction," "something," and "satisfied"?)[4]

Winnicott continues:

> Also I think there is not necessarily an integration between a child asleep and a child awake. . . . Once dreams are remembered and even conveyed somehow to a third person, the dissociation is broken down a little; but some people never clearly remember their dreams, and children depend very much on adults for getting to know their dreams. It is normal for small children to have anxiety dreams and terrors. At these times children need someone to help them to remember what they dreamed.

---

4. Of course, I am not suggesting that Winnicott planned, or even was aware of, the way he was using alliteration, syntax, rhythm, punning and so on to create specific effects in his use of language any more than a talented poet plans ahead of time which metaphors, images, rhymes, rhythms, meters, syntactical structures, diction, allusions, line lengths and so on that he will use. The act of writing seems to have a life of its own. It is one of the "rights and privileges," as well as one of the pleasures, of critical reading to try to discern what is going on in a piece of writing—regardless of whether the writer intended it or was even cognizant of it.

It is a valuable experience whenever a dream is both dreamed *and* remembered, precisely because of the breakdown of dissociation that this represents. (p. 151)

→ suggests +ve thing to understand + own dreaming + waking unconscious + conscious experiences as separate.

In this part of the paper, Winnicott speaks of how important it is for a child to have the experience of conveying his dream "somehow to a third person." Every time I read this sentence, I find it jarring and confusing. I attempt to account for a third person in the apparently two-person experience of a dream (not yet the child's creation or possession) being "conveyed somehow" to a third person. Is the third person the experience of the father's symbolic presence even in his absence? Perhaps, but such an idea seems too much an experience of the mind, disconnected from the bodily feel—the sense of aliveness—that one experiences when engaging with a child in spoken or unspoken conversation. A dream unobtrusively can be entered into a conversation or into playing, sometimes wordlessly, because the child *is* the dream before the dream is his. Thus, the three people are, from this perspective, the dreaming child, the waking child, and the adult. This interpretation is suggested by the language; but the reader, once again, must do the work of imaginatively entering into the experience of reading. The language quietly creates (as opposed to discusses) the confusion experienced by the reader/child about how many people are present in the act of conveying a dream to an adult. The reader experiences what it feels like for a child to be two people and yet not notice that experience until an adult gives him help in "getting to know . . . [what are becoming *his*] dreams" (p. 151).

"Getting to know" his dreams—the expression is uniquely Winnicott; no one else could have written these words. The phrase is implicitly a metaphor, in which an adult "makes the introductions" in the first meeting of a waking child and his dreams. In this imaginary social event, not only is the child learning that he has a dream life, his unconscious is learning that "it" (which in health is forever in the process of becoming "I") has a "waking life."

The metaphorical language of this passage carries a heavy theoretical load without the slightest evidence of strain. First of all, there is the matter that—as Freud (1915) put it—the unconscious "is alive" (p. 190), and consequently "getting to know" one's dreams is no less than the beginning of healthy communication at the "frontier" (p. 193) of the unconscious and preconscious mind. As the waking child and the dreaming child become acquainted with one another (i.e., as the child comes to experience himself as the same person who has both a waking life and a dream life), the experience of dreaming feels less strange (other to oneself) and hence less frightening.[5]

It might be said that when a dream is both dreamed and remembered, the conversation between the con-

---

5. Even as adults, we never completely experience dream life and waking life as two different forms of the experience of ourselves as one person. This is reflected in the language we use to talk about dreams. For example, we say "I had a dream last night" [it happened to me] and not "I made a dream last night."

scious/preconscious and the unconscious aspects of mind across the repression barrier is enhanced. But once it is put in these terms, the reasons for enjoying Winnicott's writing become all the more apparent. In contrast to the noun-laden language of *preconscious, conscious, unconscious, repression,* and so on, Winnicott's language seems to be all verb: "feeling something," "getting to know their dreams," "screaming," "possessed."

Winnicott then turns to the infant's experience of his earliest relations with external reality:

> In terms of baby and mother's breast (I am not claiming that the breast is essential as a vehicle of mother-love) the baby has instinctual urges and predatory ideas. The mother has a breast and the power to produce milk, and the idea that she would like to be attacked by a hungry baby. These two phenomena do not come into relation with each other till the mother and child *live an experience together.* The mother being mature and physically able has to be the one with tolerance and understanding, so that it is she who produces a situation that may with luck result in the first tie the infant makes with an external object, an object that is external to the self from the infant's point of view. (p. 152; emphasis Winnicott's)

In this passage the language is doing far more than is immediately apparent. "The baby [at this juncture] has instinctual urges and predatory ideas. The mother [with an internal life quite separate from that of the infant] has a breast and the power to produce milk, and the idea that she would like to be attacked by a hungry baby." The deadly seriousness (and violence) of these words—instinctual urges, predatory, power, attack—plays off against the whimsy and humor of the intentionally overdrawn images. The notion of a baby with "predatory ideas" conjures up images of a scheming mastermind criminal in diapers. And, in a similar way, the notion of a mother who would like to be "attacked by a hungry baby" stirs up images of a mother (her large breasts engorged with milk) walking through dimly lit alleys at night hoping to be violently assaulted by a hoodlum baby with a terrible craving for milk. The language, at once serious and playful (and at times even ridiculous), creates a sense of the complementarity of the internal states of mother and infant: a complementarity that is going on only in parallel, and not yet in relation to one another.

In the sentence that immediately follows, we find one of Winnicott's most important theoretical contributions to psychoanalysis—an idea that has significantly shaped the second fifty years of analytic thought. As the idea is rendered here, it is, to my mind, even more richly suggestive than it is in its later, more familiar forms: "These two phenomena [the infant with his predatory urges and ideas and the mother with her instinctual urges and her wish to be attacked by a hungry baby] do not come into relation with each other till the mother and child *live an experience together*" (p. 152).

"*Live an experience together*"—what makes the phrase remarkable is the unexpected word "live." The mother and child do not "take part in," "share," "participate in," or "enter into" an experience together: they live an experience together. In this single phrase, Winnicott is suggesting (though I think he is not fully aware of this as he writes this paper) that he is in the process of transforming psychoanalysis, both as a theory and as a therapeutic relationship, by altering the notion of what is most fundamental to human psychology. No longer will it be desiring and regulating desire (Freud), loving, hating, and making reparations (Klein), or object-seeking and object-relating (Fairbairn) that are of greatest importance in the development of the psyche-soma. Instead, what Winnicott is beginning to lay out here for the first time is the idea that the central organizing thread of psychological development from its inception is the experience of being alive and the consequences of disruptions to the continuity of being.

The specific way that Winnicott uses language in this passage is critical to the nature of the meanings it generates. In the phrase "live an experience together," "live" is a transitive verb, which takes "experience" as its object. Living an experience is an act of doing something to someone or something (as much as the act of hitting a ball is an act of doing something to the ball); it is an act of infusing experience with life. Human experience does not have life until we live it (as opposed to simply having it in an operational way). Mother and child do not come into relation to one another until they each *do something* to experience: that is, they live it *together* (not simply at the same time, but while experiencing and responding to each other's separate act of being alive in living the experience).

The paragraph concludes: "The mother being mature and physically able has to be the one with tolerance and understanding, so that it is she who produces a situation that may with luck result in the first tie the infant makes with an external object, an object that is external to the self from the infant's point of view" (p. 152). The unstated paradox that emerges here lies in the idea that living an experience *together* serves to *separate* the mother and infant (to bring them, from the infant's perspective, "into relation with each other" as separate entities). This paradox lies at the heart of the experience of illusion: "I think of the process as if two lines came from opposite directions, liable to come near each other. If they overlap there is a moment of *illusion*—a bit of experience which the infant can take as *either* his hallucination *or* a thing belonging to external reality" (p. 152; emphasis Winnicott's).

Of course, what is being introduced is the concept that Winnicott (1951) later termed "transitional phenomena." The "moment of illusion" is a moment of psychological "overlap" of the mother and infant—a moment in which the mother lives an experience with the infant in which she actively/unconsciously/naturally provides herself as an object that can be experienced by the infant at once as his creation (an unnoticed experience because there is nothing that is *not* what is expected) *and* as his discovery (an event with a quality of otherness in a world external to his sense of self).

In other language, the infant comes to the breast when excited, and ready to hallucinate something fit to be attacked. At that moment the actual nipple appears and he is able to feel it was that nipple that he hallucinated. So his ideas are enriched by actual details of sight, feel, smell, and next time this material is used in the hallucination. In this way he starts to build up a capacity to conjure up what is actually available. The mother has to go on giving the infant this type of experience. (pp. 152–153)

What Winnicott is attempting to describe (and succeeds in capturing in his use of language) is not simply an experience, but a *way* of experiencing that is lighter, more full of darting energy, than other ways of experiencing. The initial metaphor that Winnicott uses to introduce this way of experiencing involves the image of mother and infant as two lines (or is it lives?) coming from opposite directions (from the world of magic and from the world of grounded consensual reality), which are "liable to come near each other" (p. 152). The word "liable" is unexpected, with its connotations of chance events (perhaps of an unwelcome nature). Is there a hint of irony about accidents being a port of entry into the "real world"?

For Winnicott, the maternal provision is even more complex than the creation of a psychological/interpersonal field in which the infant gains entry at the same moment into external reality, internal reality, and the experience of illusion. The mother's task at this stage of things also involves protecting "her infant from complications that cannot yet be understood by the infant" (p. 153). "Complications" is a word newly made in this sentence. In Winnicott's hands, it takes on a rather specific set of meanings having to do with a convergence of internal and external stimuli that are related to each other in ways beyond the capacity of the infant to understand. A few years later, speaking of the mother's efforts "not to introduce complications beyond those which the infant can understand and allow for," Winnicott adds: "in particular she tries to insulate her baby from coincidences" (1949, p. 245). "Coincidences" is a word even more richly enigmatic than "complications." It is a word with a long and troubling history in Western myth and literature. (Sophocles's version of the Oedipus myth represents only one instance of the ruin that "coincidence" can leave in its wake.)

Winnicott does not explain what he means by "coincidences" or "complications," much less how one might go about insulating babies from them. His indefinite, enigmatic language does not fill a space with knowledge; it opens up a space for thinking, imagining, and freshly experiencing. One possible reading of the words "complications" and "coincidences" (as Winnicott is using/ creating them) that I sometimes find useful goes as follows: The coincidences or complications from which a baby needs to be insulated involve chance simultaneities of events that take place in the infant's internal and external realities at a time when the two are only beginning to be differentiated from one another. For instance, a hungry infant may become both fearful and rageful as he waits for his mother longer than he can tolerate. The mother may be feeling preoccupied and distraught for

reasons that have nothing to do with the infant—perhaps
as a consequence of a recent argument with her husband,
or a physical pain that she fears is a symptom of a serious
illness. The simultaneity of the internal event (the infant's
hunger, fear, rage) and the external event (the mother's
emotional absence) is a coincidence that the infant cannot understand. He makes sense of it by imagining that
it is his own anger and predatory urges that have killed
the mother. The mother who had earlier wished to be
attacked by a hungry baby is gone and in her place is a
lifeless mother, passively allowing herself to be attacked
by the hungry baby as carrion is available for consump-
tion by vultures.

"Coincidence" leads the infant defensively to bring
a degree of order and control to his experience by drawing what was becoming the external world back into his
internal world by means of omnipotent fantasy: "I killed
her." In contrast, when a mother and child are able to
"live an experience together," the vitality of the child's
internal world is recognized and met by the external
world (the mother's act of living the experience together
with him). Winnicott does not state these ideas as such,
but they are there to be found/created by the reader.

A note of caution is needed here with regard to what
license a reader may take in creating a text, and that caveat is provided by Winnicott himself. It is implicit in all
of his writing that creativity must not be valorized above
all else. Creativity is not only worthless, it is lethal (literally so, in the case of an infant) when disconnected from
objectivity—that is, from "acceptance of external reality"

re - creativity

(p. 153). An infant forever hallucinating what he needs will starve to death; a reader who loses touch with the writing will not be able to learn from it.

Winnicott's conception of the infant's earliest experience of accepting external reality is as beautifully rendered as it is subtle in content:

> One thing that follows the acceptance of external reality is the advantage to be gained from it. We often hear of the very real frustrations imposed by external reality, but less often hear of the relief and satisfaction it affords. Real milk is satisfying as compared with imaginary milk, but this is not the point. The point is that in fantasy things work by magic: there are no brakes on fantasy, and love and hate cause alarming effects. External reality has brakes on it, and can be studied and known, and, in fact, fantasy is only tolerable at full blast when objective reality is appreciated well. The subjective has tremendous value but is so alarming and magical that it cannot be enjoyed except as a parallel to the objective. (p. 153)

This is a muscular passage. After acknowledging what is already self-evident ("Real milk is satisfying as compared to imaginary milk"), the passage seems to break open mid-sentence: "but this is not the point. The point is that in fantasy things work by magic: there are no brakes on fantasy, and love and hate cause alarming effects." External reality is not simply an abstraction in these sentences; it is alive in the language. It is a felt presence in the sound of the words—for instance in the dense, cold, metallic

sound of the word "brakes" (which evokes in me the image
of a locomotive with wheels locked, screeching to a halt
over smooth iron tracks). The metaphor of a vehicle without the means to be stopped (a metaphor implicit in the
words "without brakes") is elaborated as the sentence
proceeds: " . . . love and hate cause alarming effects." Love
and hate are without a subject, thus making the metaphorical vehicle not only without brakes but also without
a driver (or engineer).

The modulating effects of external reality can be felt
in the restraint and frequent pauses in the first half of
the sentence that immediately follows: "External reality
has brakes on it [—], and can be studied and known [—],
and [—], in fact [—] . . . " (p. 153). Having been slowed,
the sentence (and the experience of internal and external reality) unfolds in a more flowing, but neither bland
nor lifeless, way: " . . . fantasy is only tolerable at full blast
when objective reality is appreciated well."

Winnicott returns to the subject of illusion again and
again in "Primitive Emotional Development," each time
viewing it from a somewhat different perspective. He is
without peer in his ability to capture in words what illusion might feel like to a baby. For instance, returning to
the subject late in the paper, he says that for illusion to
be generated, "a simple *contact* with external or shared
reality has to be made, by the infant's hallucinating and
the world's presenting, with moments of illusion for the
infant in which the two are taken by him to be identical,
which they never in fact are" (p. 154). For this to happen,
someone "has to be taking the trouble [a wonderfully

simple way to acknowledge that being mother to an infant is a lot of work and a lot of trouble] all the time [even
when she longs for an hour of sleep] to bring the world to
the baby in understandable form [without too many complications and coincidences], and in a limited way, suitable
to the baby's needs" (p. 154). The rhythm of the series of
clauses making up this sentence heaps requirement upon
requirement that the mother must meet in creating illusion for the baby. These efforts of the mother constitute
the intense backstage labor that is necessary if the infant
is to enjoy his orchestra seat in the performance of illusion. The performance reveals not a hint of the dirty grunt
work that creates and safeguards the life of the illusion.

The humor of the contrast between illusion as seen
from backstage and from an orchestra seat is I think not
at all lost upon Winnicott. The juxtaposition of the passage I just quoted (something of a job description for the
mother of a baby) and the paragraph that follows it (which
captures all of the sense of wonder and amazement a child
feels on seeing a magic show) can hardly be a coincidence:
"The subject of illusion . . . will be found to provide the
clue to a child's interest in bubbles and clouds and rain-
bows and all mysterious phenomena, and also to his interest in fluff. . . . Somewhere here, too, is the interest in
breath, which never decides whether it comes primarily
from within or without" (p. 154). I am not aware of a com-
parable expression in all of the analytic literature of the
almost translucent, mystifying quality of imaginative experience that becomes possible when the full blast of fantasy
is made safe by a child's sturdy grasp on external reality.

Concluding Comments

In this, the first of his major papers, Winnicott quietly, unassumingly, defies the conventional wisdom that holds writing to be primarily a means to an end: a means by which analytic data and ideas are conveyed to readers as telephones and telephone lines transport the voice in the form of electrical impulses and sound waves. The notion that our experiences as analysts and the ideas with which we make sense of them are inseparable from the language we use to create/convey them is an idea that some analysts strenuously resist. For them it is disappointing to acknowledge that discourse among analysts, whether written or spoken, will forever remain limited by our imprecise impressionistic (and consequently confusing and misleading) accounts of what we observe and how we think about what we do as psychoanalysts. For others, the inseparability of our observations and ideas, on the one hand, and the language we use to express them, on the other, is an exciting idea—it embraces the indissoluble interpenetration of life and art, neither preceding the other, neither holding dominion over the other. To be alive (in more than an operational sense) is to be forever in the process of making things of one's own, whether they be thoughts, feelings, bodily movements, perceptions, conversations, poems or analytic papers. No psychoanalyst's writing bears witness better than Winnicott's to the mutually dependent, mutually enlivening relationship of life and art.

References

Ammons, A. R. (1986). Poetics. In *The Selected Poems.* New York: Norton, p. 61.

Andreas-Salomé, L. (1916). Letter to Freud, April 9, 1916. In *Sigmund Freud and Lou Andreas-Salomé Letters,* ed. E. Pfeiffer and trans. W. and E. Robson-Scott. New York: Harcourt, Brace, Jovanovich, 1966, p. 42.

Appelbaum, S. (1966). Speaking with the second voice. *Journal of the American Psychoanalytic Association* 14: 462–477.

Arlow, J. (1979). Metaphor and the psychoanalytic situation. *The Psychoanalytic Quarterly* 48: 363–385.

Baird, T. (1968). Writing assignment. In *Fencing with Words: A History of Writing Instruction at Amherst College During the Era of Theodore Baird, 1938–1966,* ed. R. Varnum. Urbana, IL: National Council of Teachers of English, 1996, p. 200.

Balint, M. (1986). *The Basic Fault.* London: Tavistock.

Balkanyi, C. (1964). On verbalization. *International Journal of Psycho-Analysis.* 45: 64–74.

Bialik, H. (1931). Revealment and concealment in language. In *An Anthology of Hebrew Essays, Vol. 1.,* ed. I. Cohen and

B. Michali, trans. J. Sloan. Tel Aviv, Israel: Institute for the Translation of Hebrew Literature & Massada Publishing Co., Ltd., 1966, pp. 127–135.

Bion, W. (1962). *Learning from Experience.* New York: Basic Books.

———— (1976). *Four Discussions with W. R. Bion.* Perthshire, Scotland: Clunie Press, 1978.

Borges, J. L. (1923). *Fervor de Buenos Aires.* Privately printed. Excerpts in English in *Jorge L. Borges: Selected Poems,* ed. A. Coleman. New York: Viking, 1999, pp. 1–32.

———— (1933). The street corner man. In *The Aleph and Other Stories, 1933–1969,* ed. and trans. N. T. di Giovanni in collaboration with J. L. Borges. New York: Dutton, 1970, pp. 33–44.

———— (1941). Pierre Menard, author of the *Quixote.* In *Labyrinths: Selected Stories and Other Writings,* ed. D. Yates and J. Irby. New York: New Directions, 1962, pp. 36–44.

———— (1944). *Ficciones* [Fictions]. Buenos Aires, Argentina: Editorial Sud.

———— (1946). A new refutation of time. In *Labyrinths: Selected Stories and Other Writings,* ed. D. Yates and J. Irby. New York: New Directions, 1962, pp. 217–236.

———— (1949). *El Aleph.* Buenos Aires: Editorial Losada.

———— (1957). Borges and I. In *Labyrinths: Selected Stories and Other Writings,* ed. D. Yates and J. Irby. New York: New Directions, 1962, pp. 246–247.

———— (1960a). Poem of the gifts. In *Jorge Luis Borges, Selected Poems, 1923–1967,* trans. and ed. N. T. di Giovanni. New York: Delta, 1972, pp. 117–119.

———— (1960b). The other tiger. In *Jorge Luis Borges: Selected Poems, 1923–1967,* trans. and ed. N. T. di Giovanni. New York: Delta, 1968, pp. 129–131.

———— (1962). *Labyrinths: Selected Stories and Other Writings,* ed. D. Yates and J. Irby. New York: New Directions.

———— (1967–1968). *This Craft of Verse.* Cambridge: Harvard University Press, 2000.

———— (1970). An autobiographical essay. In *The Aleph and Other Stories, 1933–1969,* ed. and trans. N. T. di Giovanni in collaboration with J. L. Borges. New York: Dutton, 1970, pp. 203– 262.

———— (1971). Foreword. In *Jorge Luis Borges: Selected Poems, 1923–1967,* trans. and ed. N. T. di Giovanni. New York: Delta, 1972, pp. xv–xvi.

———— (1981). Poetry. In *Twenty-Four Conversations with Borges (Including a Selection of Poems). Interviews by Roberto Alifano 1981–1983,* trans. N. S. Araúz, W. Barnstone, and N. Escandell. Housatonic, MA: Lascaux Publishers, 1984, pp. 37–41.

———— (1982). Possession of yesterday. In *Twenty-Four Conversations with Borges (Including a Selection of Poems). Interviews by Roberto Alifano 1981–1983,* trans. N. S. Araúz, W. Barnstone, and N. Escandell. Housatonic, MA: Lascaux Publishers, 1984, p. 157.

———— (1984). *Seven Nights,* trans. E. Weinberger. New York: New Directions.

———— (1998). *Jorge Luis Borges: Collected Fictions,* trans. A. Hurley. New York: Viking.

———— (1999). *Jorge Luis Borges: Selected Poems,* ed. A. Coleman. New York: Viking.

Boyer, L. B. (1988). Thinking of the interview as if it were a dream. *Contemporary Psychoanalysis* 24: 275–281.

———— (1997). The verbal squiggle game in treating the seriously disturbed patient. *Psychoanalytic Quarterly* 66: 62–81.

Bridgman, P. W. (1950). Philosophical implications of physics. In *Seeing and Writing,* ed. W. Gibson. New York: McKay, 1959, pp. 148–157.

Brody, M. (1943). Neurotic manifestations of the voice. *Psychoanalytic Quarterly* 12: 371–380.

Calvino, I. (1986). *Six Memos for the Next Millennium.* Cambridge, MA: Harvard University Press.

Corcoran, N. (1986). *Seamus Heaney.* London: Faber and Faber.

Edelson, J. (1983). Freud's use of metaphor. *The Psychoanalytic Study of the Child* 38: 17–59.

Edelson, M. (1972). Language and dreams. *The Psychoanalytic Study of the Child* 27: 203–282.

——— (1975). *Language and Interpretation in Psychoanalysis.* Chicago: University of Chicago Press.

Eliot, T. S. (1924). The metaphysical poets. In *Selected Essays.* New York: Harcourt, Brace and World, 1932, pp. 241–250.

——— (1940). East Coker. In *T. S. Eliot: The Complete Poems and Plays, 1909–1950.* New York: Harcourt Brace, 1980, pp. 123–129.

Emerson, R. W. (1844). The poet. In *The Essays of Ralph Waldo Emerson.* Cambridge, MA: Harvard University Press, 1987, pp. 219–242.

Foster, T. (1989). *Seamus Heaney.* Boston: Twayne.

Freud, S. (1893–1895). *Studies in Hysteria. Standard Edition* 2.

——— (1896). Letter 52 to Fliess, June 12, 1896. *Standard Edition* 1.

——— (1900). *Interpretation of Dreams. Standard Edition* 4/5.

——— (1914a). On the history of the psycho-analytic movement. *Standard Edition* 14.

——— (1914b). Mourning and melancholia. *Standard Edition* 14.

——— (1915). The unconscious. *Standard Edition* 14.

——— (1916). Letter to Andreas-Salomé, May 25, 1916. In *Sigmund Freud and Lou Andreas-Salomé Letters,* ed. E. Pfeiffer and trans. W. and E. Robson-Scott. New York: Harcourt, Brace, Jovanovich, 1966, p. 45.

——— (1923). Two encyclopaedia articles. *Standard Edition* 18.

———— (1933). New introductory lectures on psycho-analysis XXXI: The dissection of the psychical personality. *Standard Edition* 22.

Frost, R. (1914a). Letter to John T. Barlett, February 22, 1914. In *Robert Frost: Collected Poems, Prose, and Plays*, ed. R. Poirier and M. Richardson. New York: Library of America, 1995, pp. 673–679.

———— (1914b). Mending wall. In *Robert Frost: Collected Poems, Prose, and Plays*, ed. R. Poirier and M. Richardson. New York: Library of America, 1995, pp. 39–40.

———— (1915). The imagining ear. In *Robert Frost: Collected Poems, Prose, and Plays*, ed. R. Poirier and M. Richardson. New York: Library of America, 1995, pp. 687–689.

———— (1923a). The need of being versed in country things. In *Robert Frost: Collected Poems, Prose, and Plays*, ed. R. Poirier and M. Richardson. New York: Library of America, 1995, p. 223.

———— (1923b). For once, then, something. In *Robert Frost: Collected Poems, Prose, and Plays*, ed. R. Poirier and M. Richardson. New York: Library of America, 1995, p. 208.

———— (1924). Letter to Louis Untermeyer, March 10, 1924. In *Robert Frost: Collected Poems, Prose, and Plays*, ed. R. Poirier and M. Richardson. New York: Library of America, 1995, pp. 702–704.

———— (1928a). Acquainted with the night. In *Robert Frost: Collected Poems, Prose, and Plays*, ed. R. Poirier and M. Richardson. New York: Library of America, 1995, p. 234.

———— (1928b). West-running Brook. In *Robert Frost: Collected Poems, Prose, and Plays*, ed. R. Poirier and M. Richardson. New York: Library of America, 1995, pp. 236–238.

———— (1930). Education by poetry. In *Robert Frost: Collected Poems, Prose, and Plays*, ed. R. Poirier and M. Richardson. New York: Library of America, 1995, pp. 717–728.

———— (1936). Letter to L. W. Payne, Jr., March 12, 1936. In

Selected Letters of Robert Frost, ed. L. Thompson. New York: Holt, Reinhart and Winston, 1964, pp. 426–427.

————— (1939). The figure a poem makes. In *Robert Frost: Collected Poems, Prose, and Plays,* ed. R. Poirier and M. Richardson. New York: Library of America, 1995, pp. 776–778.

————— (1942a). The most of it. In *Robert Frost: Collected Poems, Prose, and Plays,* ed. R. Poirier and M. Richardson. New York: Library of America, 1995, p. 307.

————— (1942b). Never again would birds' song be the same. In *Robert Frost: Collected Poems, Prose, and Plays,* ed. R. Poirier and M. Richardson. New York: Library of America, 1995, p. 308.

————— (1942c). I could give all to time. In *Robert Frost: Collected Poems, Prose, and Plays,* ed. R. Poirier and M. Richardson. New York: Library of America, 1995, pp. 304–305.

————— (1947). Directive. In *Robert Frost: Collected Poems, Prose, and Plays,* ed. R. Poirier and M. Richardson. New York: Library of America, 1995, pp. 341–342.

————— (1962). On extravagance: A talk. In *Robert Frost: Collected Poems, Prose, and Plays,* ed. R. Poirier and M. Richardson. New York: Library of America, 1995, pp. 902–926.

Gabbard, G. (1996). *Love and Hate in the Analytic Setting.* Northvale, NJ: Jason Aronson.

Gaddini, E. (1987). Notes on the mind-body question. *International Journal of Psycho-Analysis* 68: 315–330.

Gray, P. (1994). *The Ego and the Analysis of Defense.* Northvale, NJ: Jason Aronson.

Grotstein, J. (2000). *Who Is the Dreamer Who Dreams the Dream?* Hillsdale, NJ: Analytic Press.

Guibert, R. (1973). Jorge Luis Borges. In *Seven Voices.* New York: Knopf, pp. 77–117.

Heaney, S. (1966a). Mid-term break. In *Opened Ground: Selected Poems, 1966–1996.* New York: Farrar, Straus and Giroux, 1998, p. 11.

——— (1966b). *Death of a Naturalist*. London: Faber and Faber.

——— (1972). Belfast. In *Preoccupations: Selected Prose, 1968–1978*. New York: Farrar, Straus and Giroux, 1980, pp. 28–37.

——— (1975). Exposure. In *Opened Ground: Selected Poems, 1966–1996*. New York: Farrar, Straus and Giroux, 1998, pp. 135–136.

——— (1978). Mossbawn. In *Preoccupations: Selected Prose, 1968–1978*. New York: Farrar, Straus and Giroux, 1980, pp. 17–21.

——— (1979a). Song. In *Seamus Heaney: Selected Poems, 1966–1987*. New York: Farrar, Straus and Giroux, 1990, p. 141.

——— (1979b). The guttural muse. In *Opened Ground: Selected Poems, 1966–1996*. New York: Farrar, Straus and Giroux, 1998, p. 155.

——— (1980a). Feeling into words. In *Preoccupations: Selected Prose, 1968–1978*. New York: Farrar, Straus and Giroux, pp. 41–60.

——— (1980b). *Preoccupations: Selected Prose, 1968–1978*. New York: Farrar, Straus and Giroux.

——— (1986). The government of the tongue. In *The Government of the Tongue: Selected Prose, 1978–1987*. New York: Farrar, Straus and Giroux, 1988, pp. 91–108.

——— (1987). Clearances. In *Opened Ground: Selected Poems, 1966–1996*. New York: Farrar, Straus and Giroux, 1998, pp. 282–290.

——— (1988a). *The Government of the Tongue: Selected Prose, 1978–1987*. New York: Farrar, Straus and Giroux.

——— (1988b). *Stepping Stones*. New York: Penguin.

——— (1995). *The Redress of Poetry*. New York: Farrar, Straus and Giroux.

——— (1996). Keeping going. In *Opened Ground: Selected Poems, 1966–1996*. New York: Farrar, Straus and Giroux, 1998, pp. 375–377.

Hutter, A. (1982). Poetry in psychoanalysis: Hopkins, Rosetti, Winnicott. *International Review of Psycho-Analysis* 9: 303–316.

Ingram, D. (1996). The vigor of metaphor in clinical practice. *The American Journal of Psychoanalysis*, 56: 17–34.

James, W. (1890). *Principles of Psychology, Vol. 1*, ed. P. Smith. New York: Dover, 1950.

Jarrell, R. (1955). To the Laodiceans. In *Poetry and the Age*. New York: Vintage, pp. 34–62.

Jones, A. (1997). Experiencing language: Some thoughts on poetry and psychoanalysis. *Psychoanalytic Quarterly* 66: 683–700.

Khan, M. M. R. (1974). *The Privacy of the Self*. New York: International Universities Press.

Klein, M. (1952). Some theoretical conclusions regarding the emotional life of the infant. In *Envy and Gratitude and Other Works, 1946–1963*. New York: Delacorte, 1975, pp. 61–93.

Kohon, G. (1999). *No Lost Certainties to Be Recovered*. London: Karnac.

Lathem, E. (1966). *Interviews with Robert Frost*, ed. E. Lathem. New York: Holt, Rinehart, and Winston.

Lowell, R. (1977). Epilogue. In *Day by Day*. New York: Farrar, Straus and Giroux.

Mandelstam, O. (1933). Conversation about Dante. In *Osip Mandelstam: Complete Critical Prose*, ed. J. Harris and trans. J. Harris and C. Link. Dana Point, CA: Ardid, 1979, pp. 252–284.

Martin, J. (1983). Grief and nothingness: Loss, mourning in Robert Lowell's poetry. *Psychoanalytic Inquiry* 3: 451–484.

McDougall, J. (1974). The psychesoma and the psychoanalytic process. *International Review of Psycho-Analysis* 1: 437–459.

Meares, R. (1993). *The Metaphor of Play*. Northvale, NJ: Jason Aronson.

Ogden, T. (1986). *The Matrix of the Mind: Object Relations and the Psychoanalytic Dialogue*. Northvale, NJ: Jason Aronson.

—— (1987). The transitional oedipal relationship in female development. *International Journal of Psycho-Analysis* 68: 485–498.

—— (1989a). The initial analytic meeting. In *The Primitive Edge of Experience*. Northvale, NJ: Jason Aronson, pp. 169–194.

—— (1989b). *The Primitive Edge of Experience*. Northvale, NJ: Jason Aronson.

—— (1994a). The analytic third—working with intersubjective clinical facts. *International Journal of Psycho-Analysis* 75: 3–20.

—— (1994b). *Subjects of Analysis*. Northvale, NJ: Jason Aronson.

—— (1994c). Identificaçâo projetiva e o terceiro subjugador. *Revista de Psicanàlise de Sociedade Psicanalítica de Porto Alegre* 2: 153–162. (Published in English as "Projective identification and the subjugating third." In *Subjects of Analysis*, London and Northvale, NJ: Karnac and Jason Aronson, 1994, pp. 97–106.)

—— (1994d). The concept of interpretive action. *Psychoanalytic Quarterly* 63: 219–245.

—— (1995). Analysing forms of aliveness and deadness of the transference-countertransference. *International Journal of Psycho-Analysis* 76: 695–710.

—— (1996a). The perverse subject of analysis. *Journal of the American Psychoanalytic Association* 44: 1121–1146.

—— (1996b). Reconsidering three aspects of psychoanalytic technique. *International Journal of Psycho-Analysis* 77: 883–900.

—— (1997a). Reverie and interpretation. *Psychoanalytic Quarterly* 66: 567–595.

—— (1997b). *Reverie and Interpretation: Sensing Something Human*. Northvale, NJ: Jason Aronson.

—— (1997c). Some thoughts on the use of language in psychoanalysis. *Psychoanalytic Dialogues* 7: 1–22.

—— (1997d). Listening: Three Frost poems. *Psychoanalytic Dialogues* 7: 619–639.

Pritchard, W. (1984). *Frost: A Literary Life Reconsidered.* Amherst, MA: University of Massachusetts Press.

—— (1994). Ear training. In *Playing It by Ear: Literary Essays and Reviews.* Amherst, MA: University of Massachusetts Press, pp. 3–18.

Reider, N. (1972). Metaphor as interpretation. *International Journal of Psycho-Analysis* 53: 463–469.

Ricks, C. (1979). The mouth, the meal and the book: Review of *Fieldwork.* In *Seamus Heaney: Contemporary Critical Essays,* ed. M. Allen. New York: St. Martin's Press, 1997, pp. 95–101.

Rodriguez Monegal, E. (1978). *Jorge Luis Borges: A Literary Biography.* New York: Paragon.

Sandler, J. (1976). Dreams, unconscious fantasies and 'identity of perception.' *International Review of Psycho-Analysis* 3: 33–42.

Searles, H. (1959). The effort to drive the other person crazy— an element in the aetiology and psychotherapy of schizophrenia. In *Collected Papers on Schizophrenia and Related Subjects.* New York: International University Press, 1965, pp. 254–283.

Segal, H. (1957). Notes on symbol formation. *International Journal of Psycho-Analysis* 38: 391–397.

Shengold, L. (1981). Insight as metaphor. *The Psychoanalytic Study of the Child* 36: 289–306.

Silverman, M. (1982). Voice of conscience and sounds of the analytic hour. *Psychoanalytic Quarterly* 51: 196–217.

Steiner, G. (1989). *Real Presences.* Chicago: University of Chicago Press.

Stevens, W. (1923). The snow man. In *The Collected Poems of Wallace Stevens.* New York: Knopf, 1954, pp. 9–10.

—— (1936). The idea of order at Key West. In *The Collected*

Poems of Wallace Stevens. New York: Knopf, 1954, pp. 128–130.

———— (1947). The creations of sound. In *The Collected Poems of Wallace Stevens.* New York: Knopf, 1954, pp. 310–311.

Stoppard, T. (1999). Pragmatic theater. *The New York Review of Books,* XLVI, no. 14, Sept. 23, 1999, pp. 8–10.

Trilling, L. (1940). Freud and literature. In *The Liberal Imagination.* New York: Viking, 1952, pp. 34–57.

Tustin, F. (1986). *Autistic Barriers in Neurotic Patients.* New Haven, CT: Yale University Press.

Varnum, R. (1996). *Fencing with Words: A History of Writing Instruction at Amherst College During the Era of Theodore Baird, 1938–1966.* Urbana, IL: National Council of Teachers of English.

Vendler, H. (1984). *Wallace Stevens: Words Chosen out of Desire.* Cambridge, MA: Harvard University Press.

Winnicott, D. W. (1945). Primitive emotional development. In *Through Paediatrics to Psycho-Analysis.* New York: Basic Books, 1958, pp. 145–156.

———— (1949). Mind and its relation to the psyche-soma. In *Through Paediatrics to Psycho-Analysis.* New York: Basic Books, 1958, pp. 243–254.

———— (1951). Transitional objects and transitional phenomena. In *Playing and Reality.* New York: Basic Books, 1971, pp. 1–25.

———— (1952). Psychoses and child care. In *Through Paediatrics to Psycho-Analysis.* New York: Basic Books, 1958, pp. 219–228.

———— (1954). Metapsychological and clinical aspects of regression within the psycho-analytical set-up. In *Through Paediatrics to Psycho-Analysis.* New York: Basic Books, 1958, pp. 278–294.

———— (1958). *Through Paediatrics to Psycho-Analysis.* New York: Basic Books.

———— (1960). The theory of the parent-infant relationship. In *The Maturational Processes and the Facilitating Environment.* New York: International Universities Press, 1965, pp. 37–55.

———— (1962). The aims of psycho-analytical treatment. In *The Maturational Processes and the Facilitating Environment.* New York: Basic Books, 1965, pp. 166–170.

———— (1965). *The Maturational Processes and the Facilitating Environment.* New York: Basic Books.

———— (1971a). Playing: A theoretical statement. In *Playing and Reality.* New York: Basic Books, pp. 38–52.

———— (1971b). Playing: The search for the self. In *Playing and Reality.* New York: Basic Books, pp. 53–64.

———— (1971c). *Therapeutic Consultations in Child Psychiatry.* New York: Basic Books.

———— (1971d). *Playing and Reality.* New York: Basic Books.

Index

Thomas H. Ogden, M.D., is a graduate of Amherst College, the Yale School of Medicine, and the San Francisco Psychoanalytic Institute. He has served as an Associate Psychiatrist at the Tavistock Clinic, London, and is the Co-Founder and Director of the Center for the Advanced Study of the Psychoses. Dr. Ogden is a Supervising and Training Analyst at the Psychoanalytic Institute of Northern California and a member of the faculty of the San Francisco Psychoanalytic Institute.

Dr. Ogden is the author of *Reverie and Interpretation: Sensing Something Human*; *Subjects of Analysis*; *The Primitive Edge of Experience*; *The Matrix of the Mind: Object Relations and the Psychoanalytic Dialogue*; and *Projective Identification and Psychotherapeutic Technique*. His work has been published in more than a dozen languages.

He teaches, supervises and maintains a private practice of psychoanalysis in San Francisco.